IT'S TOO LATE. DO IT ANYWAY!

A Book About Being a Cultural Worker in the Apocalypse + a Hologram[1] Starter Kit

1 See glossary (page Δ12) for an explanation of how to use the term "hologram."

Published by Thick Press
thickpress.com
ISBN 978-1-7320666-6-3

Book design: Eleonora Toniolo
Curation: Cassie Thornton and Magdalena Jadwiga Härtelova
Writing: Cassie Thornton, Magdalena Jadwiga Härtelova, *The Hologram* community, Lita Wallis, Prem Krishnamurthy, Ruth Catlow, Amanda Nudelman, Fran Ugalde, Jennifer Bazar
Editing: Heather Kapplow and Thick Press
Proofreading: Demi Lee
Typefaces: Bastardo Grotesk by Giulia Boggio; Savon by Fanny Hamelin, Loan Bottex and Léo Guibert; Amiamie by mirat-masson; Admiral CAT by Peter Wiegel; TeX Gyre Heros by Boguslaw Jackowski and Janusz Nowacki
Photos: the curators, except pp. 35, 40, 56, 61, Field Studio Photography; pp. 48, 50, 51, 55, 58, 62–63, Fran Ugalde
Printing: hinkelsteindruck sozialistische GmbH

The texts written from the future are works of fiction. All resemblance to real events is purely coincidental.

Most of the text from "THIS IS THE EXHIBITION, this is 2038" appeared in an exhibition entitled *The Hologram*. The exhibition occurred from July 16, 2022 through May 27, 2023 at The National Museum of Psychology in Akron, Ohio as part of *FRONT International Cleveland Triennial for Contemporary Art*.

"'The Hologram' From Wikipedia, the free post-internet encyclopedia" was printed with permission from Pluto Press. A similar version, entitled "Wikipedia Entry from the Future," appeared in Cassie Thornton's *The Hologram: Feminist, Peer-to-Peer Health for a Post-Pandemic Future* (2020), published by Pluto Press as part of its Vagabonds series, edited by Max Haiven. The piece was originally commissioned by *Arts of the Working Class*.

"Hologram Manual" is based on a text originally written by Lita Wallis and Cassie Thornton, with small contributions over time from other Hologram organizers. Earlier versions appeared on the Hologram website and in print as part of *The Hologram* exhibition in Akron.

IT'S TOO LATE. DO IT ANYWAY!

CURATORS
Cassie Thornton
Magdalena Jadwiga Härtelova

CONTRIBUTORS
Cassie Thornton
Magdalena Jadwiga Härtelova
The Hologram community
Lita Wallis
Prem Krishnamurthy
Ruth Catlow
Amanda Nudelman
Fran Ugalde
Jennifer Bazar

IT'S TOO LATE. (Part One)

NOW

2038

CONTENTS

NOW

DO IT ANYWAY! (Part Two)

CONTENTS

IT'S TOO LATE.

Part One

NOW

I'M STILL HERE

Prem Krishnamurthy

I lost my mind a year ago. Not hyperbolically, but for real. Ironically enough, it was just after curating a massive contemporary art triennial focused on art as an agent of transformation, a mode of healing, and a therapeutic process.

The *FRONT International: Cleveland Triennial for Contemporary Art* was a success. Artists were able to realize powerful new works, people visited in droves, the local and international press printed pages upon pages of mostly positive ink about the exhibition. Who would have guessed that a show about healing would nearly destroy its curator?

It shouldn't have come as any surprise. Having participated in and witnessed many of these ambitious, large-scale art world endeavors, I knew that they have a penchant for burning people out. Amid their chronic idealism, such shows are typically under-staffed, under-resourced, poorly managed, too large, and operate at a breakneck pace. Even when you're aware of these pitfalls and work against them, they sneak up on you. Plus, I was trying to accomplish a quixotic task during a worldwide pandemic, when everything and everyone else was falling apart. Art folks these days talk about care all the time–as you may know, the word "curator" has the Latin "cura" for "care" at its root–but we're not always so good at practicing it.

I wish I'd had *The Hologram* on my side last summer during this exceptionally rocky patch. On paper, I did: I included Cassie

Thornton and the project in the triennial and even participated in a seven-week Hologram course a year prior. But it's telling that I never completed the final assignment: for each participant to set up their *own* Hologram. I thought it was a cute idea but skipped that part. I already knew what *The Hologram* was about and was too busy with the show anyways.

Sadly, theory isn't practice. Thinking you understand something and making it part of your life are different things. In hindsight, I wonder if having a Hologram—three other humans who cared about me enough to talk to me regularly and make sure that I had a framework of support and a sense of continuity in my mental, physical, and social well-being—would have helped me to stay grounded throughout the process, to figure out realistic boundaries, to ask for help from others when it was most needed. Perhaps I could have swerved to avoid the oncoming mental health trainwreck, or at least slowed down the impact.

Thankfully, I'm still here. And the future's still ahead. What if all the other utopian, motivated, and exhausted art workers I know had Holograms in the future? What if we each had a crew of three to keep us buoyed in bumpy times? What would the art world look like in 2028 or 2038 or beyond?

I don't plan to curate a triennial again anytime soon, but, for better or for worse, someone else surely will. I think I'll give them a copy of this book and suggest they start practicing now.

New York, 14 July 2023

What if we each had a crew of three

to keep us buoyed

in bumpy times?

NOW

TOO LATE

Cassie Thornton

As we finish the texts in this book, it has been a few years since the *FRONT International: Cleveland Triennial for Contemporary Art* opened. It seems a bit ridiculous to be composing a book about an exhibition that has long been washed away by the short-term memory of art, politics, and culture. Since the exhibition took place, the world has experienced rapid social, political, and ecological shifts. We are now living through one year of genocide in Palestine. We've also experienced more than two and a half years of a continuous war in Ukraine. My friend got her period for the first time in six years after cancer treatment. A huge earthquake took place across Turkey and Northern Syria. The summer of 2024 was the hottest on record in many places around the world. I left my marriage and am now part of a Family Abolition Reading and Action Group. The Amazon Rainforest is on fire, the worst in three decades. Amazon.com, Inc. is transforming healthcare with AI. Soon we may not need people to work at hospitals.

As mentioned earlier, I worked with Prem on a big exhibition in 2022 as part of the *FRONT* triennial. Afterwards, I asked some of my closest friends and collaborators, most of whom practice *The Hologram*, to help me reflect on being a cultural worker in the apocalypse and the tensions between making art about care and practicing care. After two years, we are still reflecting. I'm not sure if that is a sign of privilege or a sign of service, or both. If going slow is a privilege offered to me as a beneficiary of empire, I'll take it. Maybe the only good gift foisted on the white and white-adjacent members of a given intellectual European scene is the option to stop and take time to learn from our past decisions.[1] Reflection may still be one of the only ways to add the friction necessary to decelerate the high-speed-train-to-nowhere continuously produced by racial capitalism and boarded by utopian culture-makers just trying to survive.

The notion of looking back is embedded in the project I produced for the triennial. In it, I developed an exhibition that went forward to the future, to the year 2038 (when The Internet ended), in order to look back at the recent past. Now I wonder if I ever really returned.

From the beginning, I wasn't completely sure if I should accept the invitation to participate in a triennial (see my friend and collaborator Magda's closing text on page 120). My past self, the self who wanted to be a famous artist, was excited! Before the pandemic, I still wanted to be a famous artist. But after the COVID-19 pandemic revealed a global care crisis at systemic and personal levels, and I began to trust the potential value of *The Hologram* as a tool for distributing care, I changed. In 2022, the idea of focusing on exhibiting in the art world, rather than practicing and teaching *The Hologram* project, felt like recidivism; this is because *The Hologram* community was working so hard to pull our collectively held project out of the closed-off art world that only theorizes and rarely practices the ideas it theorizes. I wanted all my attention directed towards placing *The Hologram* directly into the hands of people working and struggling to live on a burning planet.

But out of admiration for my friend Prem, and because the context he offered me was so particular, I accepted the invitation.

Prem proposed holding *The Hologram* exhibition inside The Drs. Nicholas and Dorothy Cummings Center for the History of Psychology in Akron, Ohio. The mission of the museum is "to promote the history of psychology and related human sciences to the broadest community possible. The Archives actively acquires, preserves and provides access to primary sources and rare materials that support the complete historical record of psychology and related human sciences."[2] *The Hologram*, a viral mutual aid practice and community that I have been working on since 2016 (with many collectives and individual people around the world), is an alternative practice to, and a direct critique of, neoliberal therapy (therapy that is about symptom reduction for the sake of preserving an individual's ability to work to survive financially to protect the predatory economy that also makes us sick) and self-help–just two of the evil stepchildren of psychology as a field. It felt like such an honor to have *The Hologram* displayed as a part of the history, the trajectory, and ultimately the erosion of the field of psychology.

In the museum's mostly permanent exhibition, visitors walked in a loop, which was arranged chronologically and thematically: Freud, the Stanford Experiments, and other historical moments. For a year beginning in May of 2022, the last display that viewers saw was a room dedicated to *The Hologram*. When they entered this room, the lights were dim, and the walls a deep purple. There was a red dotted line across the floor in the doorway, marking the threshold of the exhibition. On one side of the dotted line, it said "2022," and on the other side it said "2038." As you crossed this line, you walked into the future. The puddles of water on the floor of the future were based on scientific predictions of regional flooding for Ohio made in 2022. All the materials on display seemed either homemade or as if they were lent by the staff of the museum. Why were there sandbags holding the shelves in place? Had the wind and water entered the museums of the future?

The version of 2038 that I devised for the exhibition was a boring rendition of a future that technology did not save. Unsurprising and subtle changes due to climate change and economic collapse were visible in the fragile infrastructure of the very homemade-looking exhibition. Within the year 2038, visitors found themselves looking at a meta-display (not a display by Facebook, I mean a display within a display) called The Great Isolation of 2020. From the vantage point of their 2038 selves (16 years older than when they arrived at the museum), visitors saw a life-size diorama of the bedroom of a person living in lockdown during the COVID-19 pandemic. There were empty Amazon boxes, motivational posters, masks and COVID tests, books on the floor and under the bed, and lots of little artifacts from a person who was exploring meanings and practices of mutual aid and social justice.

Reflection may
still be one
of the only ways
to add the friction
necessary to decelerate
the high-speed-train-to-nowhere
continuously
produced
by racial capitalism
and boarded
by utopian culture-makers just trying
to survive.

On the bed were a few pamphlets about *The Hologram*. A video showed a pre-recorded Hologram practice in session, which the character living in the room must have been watching or participating in. Their notebooks strewn about showed that they were doing some personal exploration, that their consideration of care and politics wasn't only theoretical. They were a person in a changing world, who was trying to change themselves too. *Was it fast enough? Was it already too late?*

How I answer these questions for myself depends on how much coffee I've had on a particular day. It turns out that in the apocalypse everything takes much longer than it should. When you sit in a comfortable seat as the world burns, when things are much worse than they appear, it takes a lot of time and attention to drown out the grief and guilt in order to do your "work"–even when your work is fun. And thus everything always feels a bit slow, like nothing is enough. It's as if every day is another missed opportunity to save something from extinction, murder, erasure, or loss. Again and again, we miss our chance.

Maybe the root of my impatience comes from my name. My mother named me Cassandra, after a hot actress from a soap opera called *One Life to Live*. Cassandra was also a castrated prophet from Ancient Greek mythology who predicted the Trojan War and her own death. Cassandra knew the future, but due to the patriarchy (also sometimes called Apollo), no one believed her. My engine runs on caffeinated prophesying, nervous but sharp, making me furiously aware of my one life to live. As temperatures rise and environmental and social crises occur more frequently, I drink more coffee and get closer to the future at an accelerated rate, scanning for death. My caffeine high fades, my attention has been spent visiting a future I fear, and all I know is that endings will not be avoided in the future.

I don't think the culture industry will be the one to offer a solution to humanity's current multi-faceted dilemmas. And at the same time, even as a small artist who knows better, I do feel a pressure to transform quicker, to save something, to have an answer. It is too late for that, because we know better than to believe in heroes or simple solutions. But I don't think we are ever too late to begin long processes of collective transformation. The thing I love about long social processes is that they make it impossible to predict the outcome. Time and causality are not variables that anyone can control or understand, not even a tardy caffeinated prophet.

And here it is over two years after the conclusion of the exhibition, and I am only now writing this text! Is *this* too late? It took all of us so many months to find time to write a text for this book, too. Why are we working so much? Why don't we have time and space to reflect on our work more often? Why can't we make time to write funny texts together when we are, in fact, the people who have won the most luxurious and free lifestyles that our sick empire has to offer? We, as academics, artists, and culture makers, are *supposedly* free to do what we want to do. But as financially precarious, disabled, sick, and alienated people in a world on fire, in what ways are we free? What is it that we want to do with the resources that we do have (which are never equally distributed)? When you ask most utopian artists or hopeless and overworked academics on the left, you get a sense that what we most want is to change this horrible world. We want to do good work that shifts the course of history. We want to know that our work matters and that it is not too late. But we are often too busy or too distracted to get to this.

This book uses my participation in the *FRONT International: Cleveland Triennial for Contemporary Art* to think through what kinds of work (utopian world-building art) is worth doing while living in the apocalypse. How many ideas, experiences, and symbols that use the rhetoric of radical politics (including care, interspecies cooperation, revolution, and environmental sustainability) are devoted more to a marketable spectacle than to actual transformation? Within these conditions, we interject *The Hologram*, a long-term social practice that anyone can use. We think it can exist as a place and time to practice more than theorize how we use our time.

Berlin, 2024

NOTES

1 It's the year 2024, I am in Berlin, and so it feels important to add: Just because we are offered this chance to reflect on history, doesn't mean we do it to produce justice. Take for example, Germany's blinding support for Israel to commit the current genocide in Palestine, and the murder of tens of thousands of Palestinians *justified by* a desire to honor the memory of Germany's *first* Holocaust.

2 "Vision, Mission, and Values," Cummings Center for the History of Psychology, accessed November 21, 2024, uakron.edu/chp/educationtest/about-us/mission.dot.

TIME TRAVEL: A SPELL

Ruth Catlow, Prem Krishnamurthy,
and Amanda Nudelman

We bow our heads, close
our eyes. See the darkness.

We raise our heads and open
our eyes. We hold our hands in
front of our chest, palms up.

There in your right hand
is yourself as you are
now. See how you feel,
what you look like.

How much money is in
your bank account?

What did you eat today?
Where is your mother?

Turn your attention to the
palm of your left hand.

There you are, sitting
or standing in 2038.

How do you look?
What languages do you speak?

What have you lost?

What kind of footwear
do you need today?

How differently do you feel?

Have these two yous
turn to each other with
a friendly curiosity.

Very slowly, bring your palms
together to clasp your hands.

We are going to rub our
hands until we feel an
intense heat build up. And
then, we're going to clap.

Now we dwell in between
time zones: present time
and the year 2038.

With our palms still together
and our eyes open, we're
going to turn from our hips
towards the right to look
into your present time.

Take a moment's breath there.

What did you learn
about survival there?

What were your most
important tools?

Where did you get
your vegetables?

Send a thank you to this
place and time for making
you exactly who you are.

Then we bring our clasped
hands in a steady curve
above our heads, centered,
and look up at the cleft
between past and future.

Then, again turning from
our hips, we face to the
left as we bring our hands
down in front of us to look
directly into the future.

Breathe the air in 2038.

What do you know when you
are there that helps you survive?

Where is your mother?

What kind of hairstyle
do you have?

We give gratitude for the
ways this place and time
allows us to know and be.

As we finish our journey,
we bow our heads and
close our eyes.

Feel the matter in your body
as it has been rearranged
from past to future.

We are grateful that we
have survived the journey.
Now, we lift our heads
and open our eyes.

We have arrived in 2038.

You've entered a new timezone!

it's 2038

THE 2038 PROBLEM

written by Cassandra, the part of Cassie that lives in the future

In the first two decades of the 2000s, many men on The Internet talked about how, on January 19, 2038, millions of the world's computer systems and smart devices would suddenly be unable to tell time. From where I am, I can tell you they were right.

When I was young in the 2020s, experts and men loved to talk about the massive consequences of a time computing problem called The 2038 Problem that would leave some computer systems unable to represent dates. They described a magical chaos that would allow something described as smart to be made *vulnerable*. What they didn't mention was that when all our devices stopped computing time, 2038 would be the very last year that we counted at all. Of course, time did not stop. But when our tech overlords stopped organizing time, we lost track of it, and everything changed. So, what the men on The Internet predicted about 2038 was true, and then some.

In the first part of the earliest era of 2038, all the things that controlled us, broke. Banks could no longer dispense money or make transactions, and their security systems went down. Cell phones stopped making calls and stopped tracking fertility or reminding you to eat breakfast. Dating apps? Done. Tons of home alarm systems went nuts and stopped telling you if your neighbors were stealing your Amazon packages. GPS-based navigation systems, such as on aircraft, ships, and road vehicles, stopped communicating location information with GPS receivers, and the drones could not target their attacks. Logistics systems around the world lost track of where to send all the goods in trucks. I remember reading about this on The Internet (RIP), fantasizing about people accessing their needs by raiding the back of a lost, abandoned truck instead of continuing to pay corporations for everything they should have already been able to access.

Back in the 2020s when I was reading about The 2038 Problem, this breakdown of society sounded like heaven in comparison to the austerity, corporate control, poverty, loneliness, self-centered avoidance, and isolation we were living–a Jeff Bezos hallucination of a seamless world produced by frictionless logistics.

We knew that, in using the exact tools that destroyed the planet in the first place, we weren't moving towards a "better" future. But we couldn't break that cycle by choice; we needed somebody or something to take away our technological toys, toys that were produced by extraction, big tech, and war. The breakdown we've endured since 2038 has forced us to remake everything in a very different way than I had ever known: without the same ticking caffeinated digital forward momentum towards the future. Without even the simplest internet apps, suddenly the next day, the next week, the next year stopped being such a big deal. Now every day is just another day sometime in 2038. Without all the technology we used to keep us on the clock, we aren't going anywhere so quickly.

Nothing is easy for us now, as we have to rebuild ourselves as well as our ways of living. For example, when The Internet stopped, a lot of people lost their memory of the world. It caused a real mental health crisis as many people had to remember their personal and collective memories without the help of "smart" devices. With waves of never-before-seen confusion and depression, a massive number of people experienced a feeling of being lost or "untethered" with nothing to plug into. This is where *The Hologram* practice came in. Those who already knew the practice began to use it more than ever, and it began to spread much more quickly.

Thanks to a network of Pirate Librarians, we preserved some of the knowledge that was previously held on The Internet. These librarians produced the Memory of the World server network with a free membership plan that anyone could join, where you could download memories from the servers that stored most of what was on The Internet. In most cities around the world, you can find a Pirate Librarian if you ask around. I didn't realize it until recently, but the Memory of the World and its Pirate Librarians had been there all along, as early as early as 2012.

Memory of the World librarians are unofficial archivists of The Internet, and they usually have a huge hard drive where they hold a nearly comprehensive download of The Internet as it stood on January 18, 2038 (the day The 2038 Problem arrived). When someone wants to look something up (remember the way we used to use "Google" *as a verb?!*) they go to their local Pirate Librarian with a USB thumb drive, and they receive a comprehensive list of sources (printed on paper) to choose from (using a pen). The Pirate Librarian then downloads the selected sources to the thumb drive. If someone wants to update the archive of The Internet, they are also welcome to provide an update to a Pirate Librarian on a USB thumb drive. The librarians travel regularly to a larger server, where updates are uploaded. That is also the place where a Pirate Librarian can go to get the most recent updates to the larger World Memory.

Eventually I began to remember things, to think clearly, and to navigate my territory without GPS—but only after months without my phone or computer. And I've been remembering how, from within the Great Isolation of COVID-19, this hypothetical future collapse of systems felt very exciting to me. But back then it also did not feel real enough for me to believe in or trust; from my safe little 2020 bedroom everything felt like a simulation.

Now I remember viscerally how during COVID, there were movements to demand the end of absurd human projects like charging rent for housing. For some, a pause in our normal lives allowed us to question whether we wanted to continue to go to work at exploitative "bullshit" jobs for very little pay. Many people also took notice of what happened when, over many years, governments divested from social services and healthcare—leaving the duties of care to be performed within the family household. Some even felt that this social equation caused a hostage crisis for both caregivers and the people receiving care–as caregiving was hidden between the home and the hospital–and other forms of care between people became less and less common, placed behind the firewall of the nuclear family. Alongside that combination of queries, I think we next asked, *what is our real work in this world, beyond wages and reputations, when everything we have been taught to do and believe is so inappropriate in the wake of societal collapse?*

Back then, that moment of possibility passed as quickly as it arrived. But I remember, with a soft nostalgic glow, living in London and wondering if the pandemic and the time we had alone during The Great Isolation could be the time when we decided to reorganize society, starting with housing and healthcare. I was ready for the social and economic devastation of a pandemic to destroy our attachment to toxic systems, for example investor-led healthcare industries and real estate markets. This energy was the spirit that went into *The Hologram* as it grew and wove people into a support system throughout the pandemic.

I wondered if there was some way that creating intentional, consensual interdependence could produce a revolutionary form of destruction, rebirthing us out of seamless logistics and into some life-loving world economy. In the years after the formally acknowledged era of the pandemic, *The Hologram* became a pedagogy and a practice that many hundreds of people used across the globe. Meanwhile the world got worse and worse. My comrades and I taught Hologram workshops online and in person as we practiced it ourselves, as we experienced the collapse of many worlds. We practiced anyway, as we waited for the moment(s) when we would feel so supported that we could not avoid our fate; to dismantle the world and remake it in a new form. And that is why I am still wondering, why did we allow ourselves to be distracted by questions of fame, of being seen in the art world, of producing exhibitions that took us away from practicing? Why didn't we realize that we could wish for more than acclaim? Why didn't we realize we could have bigger wishes? Why did it take us so long to unbrainwash ourselves, to hold sacred our dreams that the most revolutionary work we could do was to ensure that all caregivers were cared for, and to watch the dominoes fall as we slowly moved towards that wish?

This section is written by Cassie Thornton, who pretended it was 2038 so they could create, visit, and write about the exhibition at The Cummings Center for the History of Psychology in Akron, Ohio. Sometimes, it seems like a part of Cassie got stuck in the future, because now we get these strange dispatches from Cassandra through Wikipedia. But while Cassandra resided in the future, for everyone else, this exhibition opened on May 22, 2022, and closed on May 1, 2023. It was a part of *FRONT International: Cleveland Triennial for Contemporary Art*, curated by Prem Krishnamurthy. Francisca Beatriz Ugalde, curator, and Jennifer L. Bazar, Assistant Director at The National Museum of Psychology, provided huge support with installation and editorial work for the exhibition. They both traveled to 2038 with Cassie.

The following objects, descriptions, and ideas are meant to capture aspects of The Great Isolation of 2020, which emerged from our collective response to COVID-19, recorded by Cassie. The objects were located inside a diorama of a bedroom, under a big title text that read: The Great Isolation of 2020. In order to access this display about a person through a model of their bedroom in the year 2020, viewers had to cross over a line that brought them into the year 2038. When they crossed this timeline, viewers arrived in the future. While standing in 2038, they viewed a diorama about the year 2020. This diorama was lifted off the ground to prevent water damage due to flooding that is predicted to happen in 2038.

The chat bubbles here are a discussion between Francisca Beatriz Ugalde, curator, and Jennifer L. Bazar, Assistant Director at The National Museum of Psychology. Fran and Jenn worked so closely with Cassie on the exhibition that they accidentally arrived in 2038 for the duration of the exhibition. This exchange occurred over a year after the exhibition opened, while Fran and Jenn were looking through the images of the exhibition, and reflecting on how people responded.

THIS IS THE EXHIBITION

Cassie Thornton, Fran Ugalde,
and Jennifer Bazar

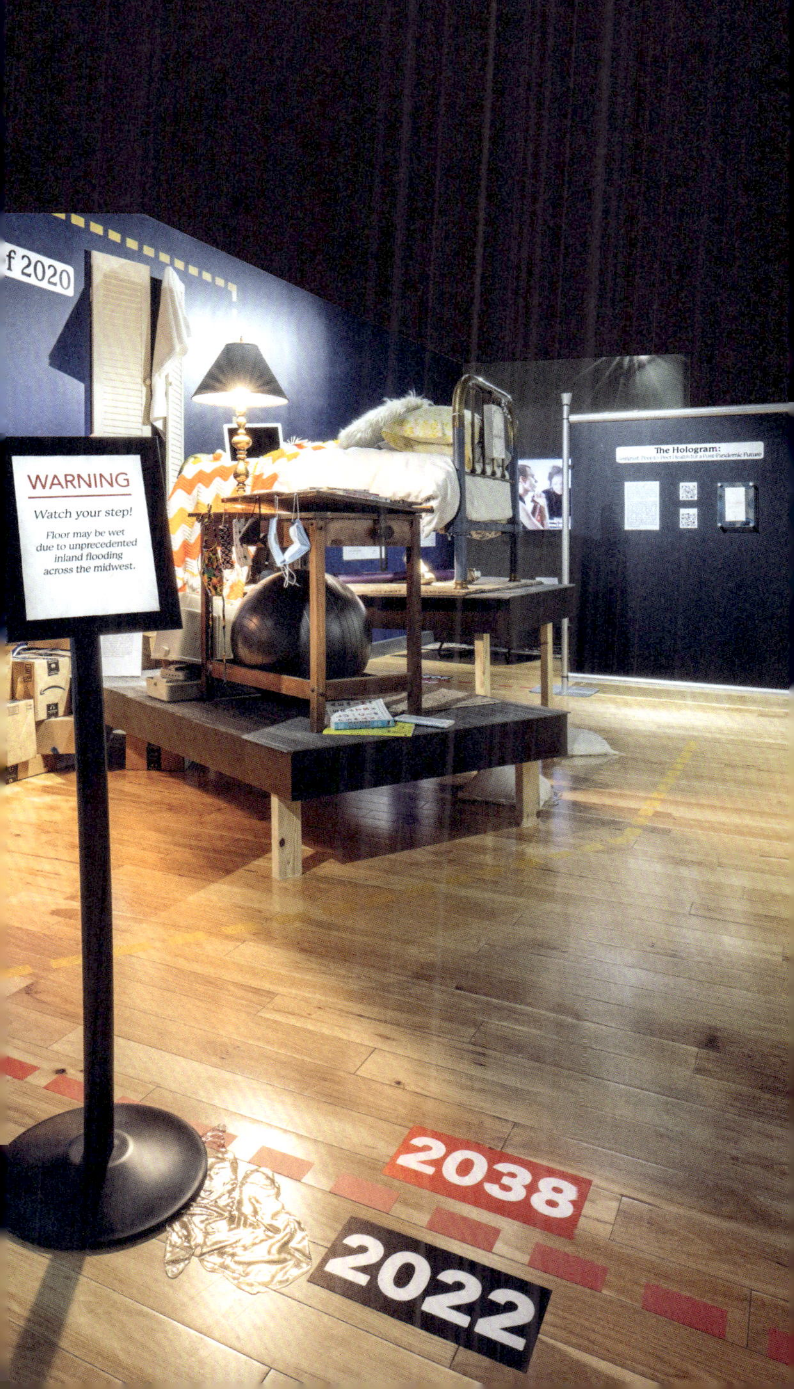

WARNING: Watch your step!

Jennifer Bazar

Fran Ugalde

I can't believe it's already time to close the exhibit!

I know, it feels like our first *Hologram* practice was just yesterday.

Do you remember our initial reactions to the exhibit proposal?

I do! We had so many concerns about integrating the exhibit into the National Museum of Psychology and how our visitors might understand an immersive story about something that started out as art and which is now a regular healthcare tool used by people around the world.

As a historian, I remember being especially worried about the risk of looking like we were offering health advice.

Yeah, working hand-in-hand with Cassie, who was intimately involved with *The Hologram*, really helped to make everything clear for the exhibition design and how to relay the message to our visitors. The distance between an abstract concept and its physical manifestation is immense.

Floor may be wet

due to unprecedented inland flooding across the midwest.

I'm so grateful the Museum was willing to allocate the little budget we had to build these platforms to keep the display materials safe from flooding. I'm always happy to loan my personal items, but I really didn't want to see my things damaged.

I still find it hard to accept that we have to think about these details while planning exhibits now. The flooding in Northeast Ohio has become so prevalent in recent years!

→ → Welcome to 2038. During your visit you are invited to view a simulated bedroom of a person living in The Great Isolation of 2020 caused by the COVID-19 pandemic. During this time, 18 years ago, people spent months or even years in their homes while others were forced into isolation on the street. 2020 was also defined by waves of climate crisis, growing wealth inequality, racist violence, and worldwide street protests.

With a growing awareness of the unjust and inhumane systems that led to the crises, mutual aid groups rose up during The Great Isolation. One of these was *The Hologram*, a peer-to-peer support network that offers an online or in-person practice. This practice is based on the idea that every person's health is dependent on the health of the people in their lives, and vice versa. In 2038 *The Hologram* is more important than ever as we strive to make a world where everyone is valued and well cared for.

Our thanks to the staff at the National Museum of Psychology for scavenging supplies to create this exhibition after the mass public cuts to museums last year.

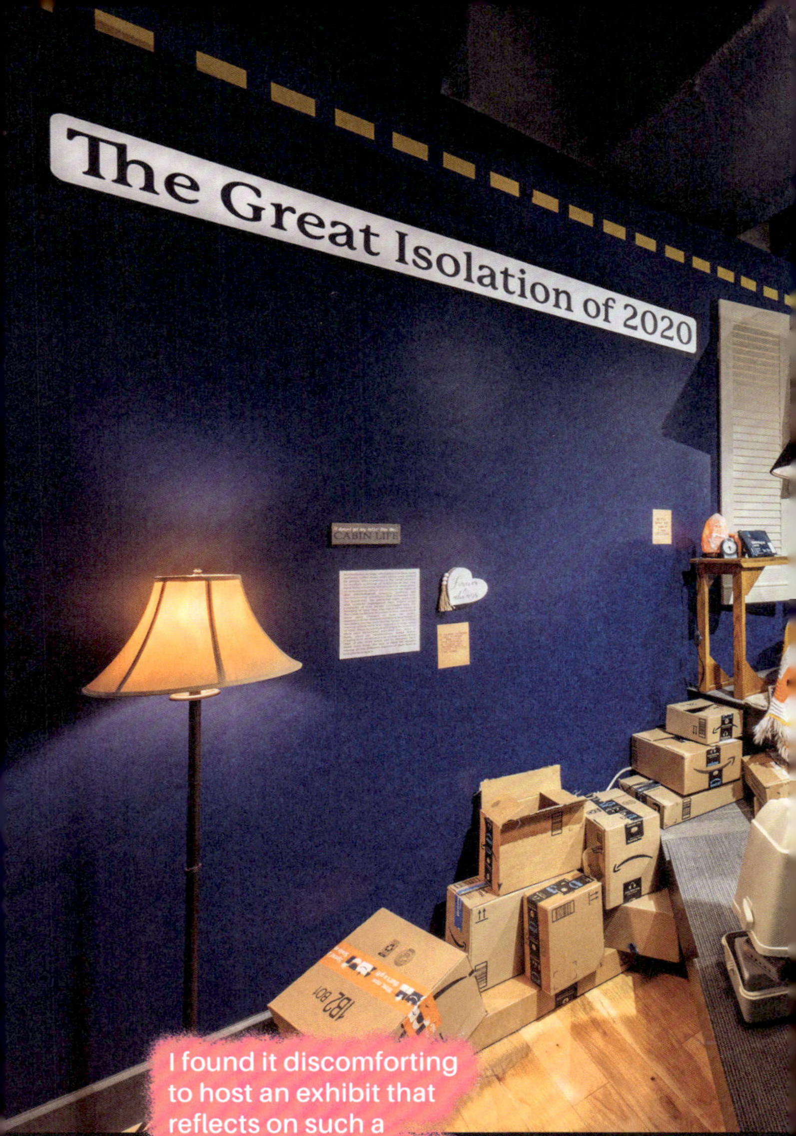

I found it discomforting to host an exhibit that reflects on such a challenging time from our shared, lived history. And yet there was also a comfort in the familiarity. The Great Isolation raised so many different emotions in all of us.

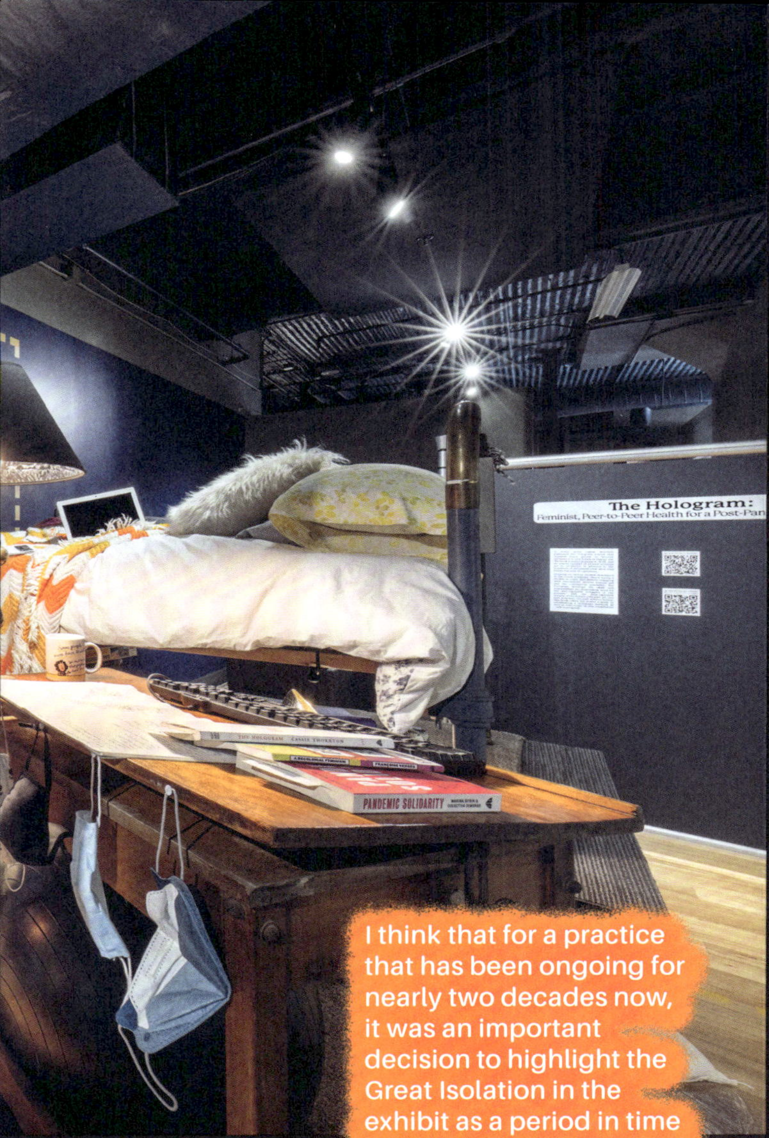

I think that for a practice that has been ongoing for nearly two decades now, it was an important decision to highlight the Great Isolation in the exhibit as a period in time in which we were allowed to imagine what having time looked like. It was important that our visitors understood that *The Hologram* really ballooned out of the fact that we were all forced to stop and hit pause on our lives.

HOW WE ALL BECAME CAREGIVERS

Nonlinear, Speculative US Timeline: 2020-2038

→

The timeline, originally finely cut out of masking tape, was produced by Cassie Thornton in 2022 through conversations with design researcher Nadine Botha. Cassie (Cassandra) outlined possible large-scale changes that could take place in the US between the years of 2020 and 2038. Based on real corporate and governmental forecasts, the timeline anticipated a future when multiple environmental, social, and economic factors necessitate more care for more people than ever. And look at us now! Whenever you are reading this!

2038

I love that a timeline was included in the exhibit design. It ended up being a really helpful tool to contextualize the development and adaptation of *The Hologram* for our visitors.

Yeah, it also made me reflect on the personal impacts these events have had. I'm not sure I would have been able to take this project on without access to Universal Basic Income. It allowed me the emotional and time commitments needed to bring this project to life.

Cancellation of student debt: For hundreds of thousands of students, trillions of dollars in debt to the US Department of Education are forgiven, and public funding for US universities ends.

Continued violence against racialized people: Causes deepening nationwide conversation and policy change moving towards police and prison abolition, but there is also racist backlash.

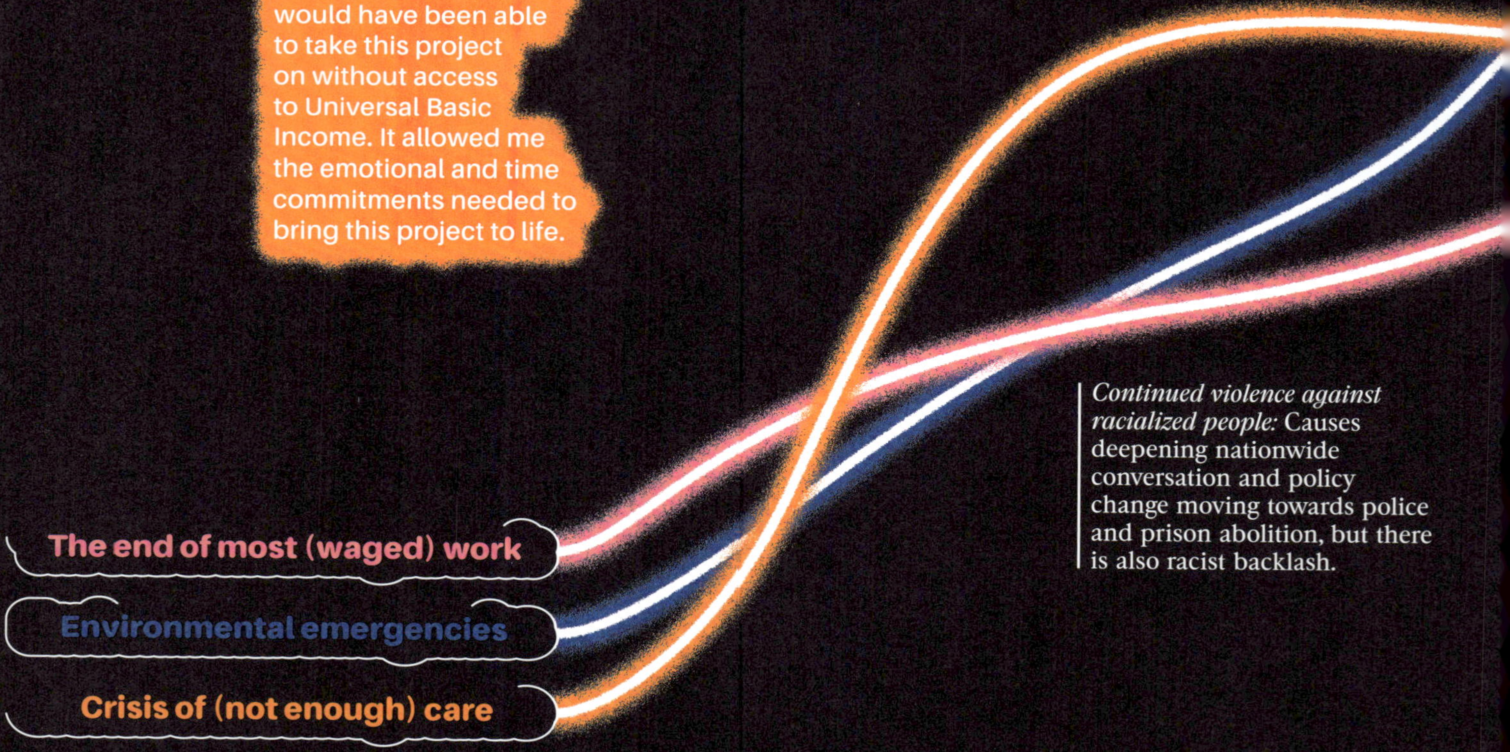

2038

←

THE GREAT ISOLATION OF 2020

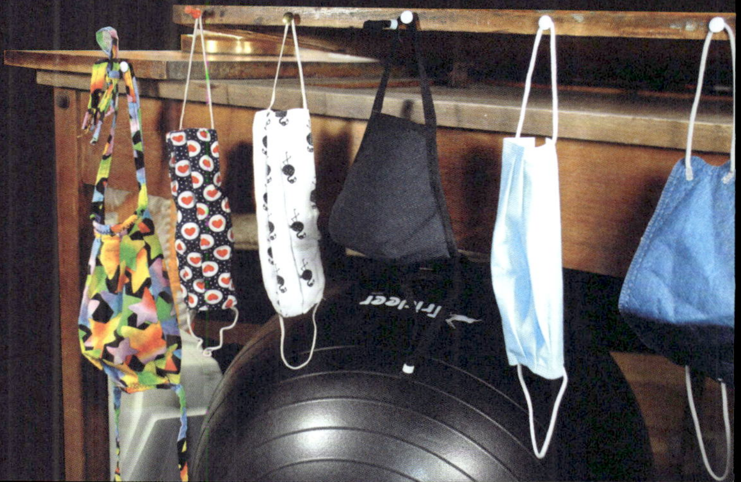

Unprecedented number of aging, sick, and differently abled people: Produces a booming home health industry, lots of new forms of small and large private clinics, and a deficit of skilled care workers.

Single Payer Healthcare achieved in the US: Run privately with telemedicine by artificial intelligence, drones, and low wage workers. The world's first fully automated hospital is established.

Growing numbers of climate and war refugees: Means a growing number of people seek housing, education, and healthcare in the US.

Universal Basic Income is implemented: Making wage work less common and offering free time for many (former) wage workers, while public services like education and welfare are cut.

Extreme heat, inland flooding and summer droughts increase exponentially in Ohio: Where there are more than 320,000 people 65 and older, or under five years old, living below the poverty line.

So much has changed since the Great Isolation. I forget that we didn't always have access to Universal Basic Income, what a difference it has made!

← It was forbidden for people in some jurisdictions to see other people during parts of the pandemic in 2020. In certain places, people were not even allowed to take a walk together outdoors, and many people didn't hug their family members (from other households) for YEARS. For sanctioned social situations like going to the grocery store, or getting a COVID test, masks were required. Towards the beginning of the pandemic, homemade masks were used, many handsewn or made on sewing machines using scraps of fabric in the homes of people during The Great Isolation. Later, these types of masks were replaced by scientifically-tested, store-bought N95 masks. Some people who self-identified as introverts even enjoyed the anonymity provided by the mask; others could be seen driving alone wearing a mask, safe from themselves.

I think the masks were one of the most talked about and polarizing details in the exhibit. I feel like every visitor had an opinion they wanted to share, either how much they hated them, or how much they appreciated them. I didn't expect to hear so many stories about face masks!

Personally, I loved it when your mom visited and asked for a photo of her posing next to the sewing machine she loaned for display—it was this great moment that reminded me how intimately connected we are to these objects and to this history.

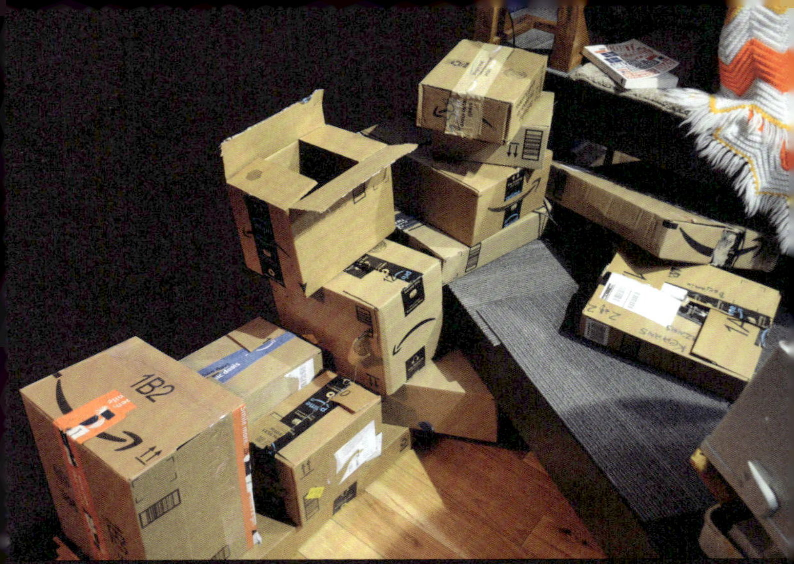

↑ In 2020, those who were able to work from home worked more hours and attended more meetings than ever. Because of lockdowns and fear of COVID exposure, many people relied on delivery services for all their household needs. It is estimated that companies delivered 4.2 billion parcels in one year:[1] Imagine the amount of cardboard that piled up! What do you think happened to all that packaging? What do you think happened to all those delivery people?

I'm amazed you saved all these boxes! What a huge amount of waste the at-home delivery system produced...

Oh, you know I save absolutely everything—that's how we keep our expenses low!

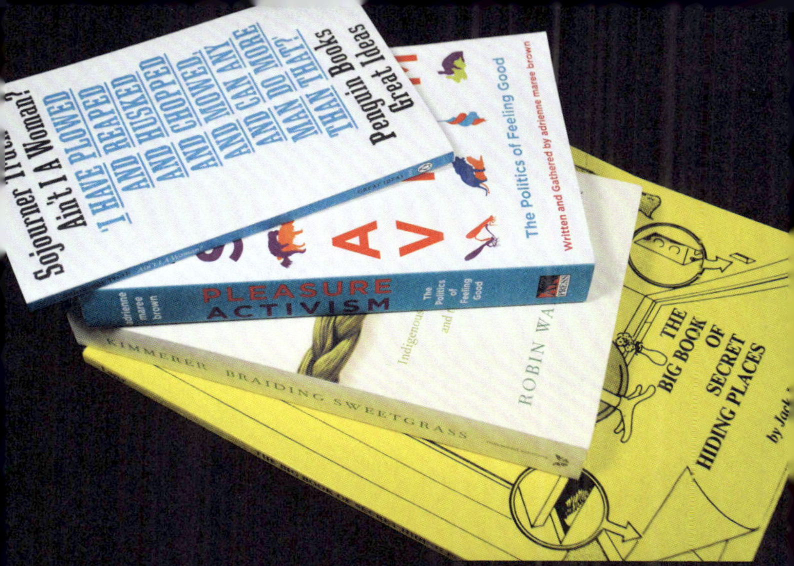

↑ During The Great Isolation, many people turned towards the entertainment of an old technology, print books. While there was a dip in sales of self-help and travel books, they were temporarily replaced with books about social justice. A correlation has been made between this trend in social justice book publishing and the growing sense of interdependence (you can't be healthy if those around you are sick or otherwise unwell) people experienced during COVID. (As well as with the large uprisings that took place around the world demanding racial justice after the murder of George Floyd.)

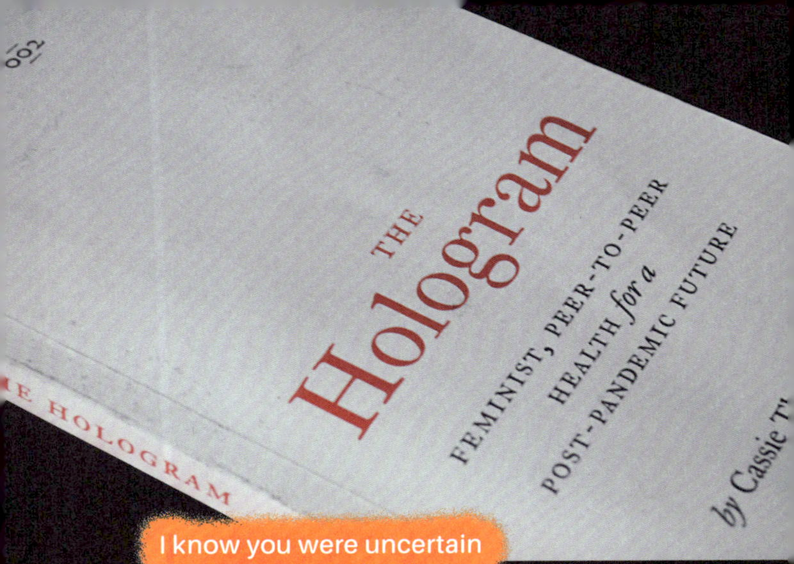

I know you were uncertain about how an exhibit about *The Hologram* would fit within the National Museum of Psychology. How do you feel now?

I find it hard to believe I was ever so hesitant! *The Hologram* provided the perfect bookend: the Museum opens with a display about the development of the modern mental health care system through the establishment of asylums and state hospitals and then ended with an installation about the development of *The Hologram* as a feminist, peer-to-peer health care practice. They complimented each other perfectly.

2038

← In 2020, artist Cassie Thornton published *The Hologram*, a book that inspired many people to become interested in new forms of mutual aid. The book remains popular in 2038, and an untold number of pirated versions are in circulation in addition to the hundreds of thousands that were sold before the unplugging of capitalism (also known as The 2038 Problem).

Drawing on radical models developed in the Greek solidarity clinics during a decade of crisis, and directly engaging with discussions around mutual aid and the COVID-19 pandemic, *The Hologram* develops the skills and relationships we desperately need for the anti-capitalist struggles of the moment, and the post-capitalist society of the future. One part art, one part activism, one part science fiction, this book offers the reader a guide to establishing a Hologram network as well as reflections on its cooperative work in progress.

→ Motivational sayings, often placed on faux wood surfaces, coffee mugs, and t-shirts were utilized by people who experienced The Great Isolation to mediate a feeling of helplessness that may have been occurring due to a lack of information or assuredness about the future in the midst of dire psychological, financial, political, and environmental conditions associated with the pandemic. The particular signs, postcards, and trinkets highlighted here reflect some examples of how people contended with the bending of time that was reported by many in The Great Isolation. In a state of flux, when there were daily changes to how the public understood the disease and thus a deep sense of instability for the near and far future, an infinite waiting *mixed with fear* created a strange sense of time. Many housed people began to devise their own structured activities (i.e., wine at 6 p.m., pizza on Wednesdays, walks before logging in to work) as a way to stay aware of the days of the work week and to separate their work time from the rest of their life despite all the different aspects of their lives occurring in one physical space.

→ → For many who lived within The Great Isolation, sleep became important, but difficult. Reports of mass sleeplessness by women began in 2020 when temperatures rose, thanks to climate change. It was also speculated that sleep action disorder became common during lockdown, wherein dreamers began to act out their dreams while in bed. Widespread advice was to keep sharp or heavy objects away from the bed, or for people to sleep separate from their partners.

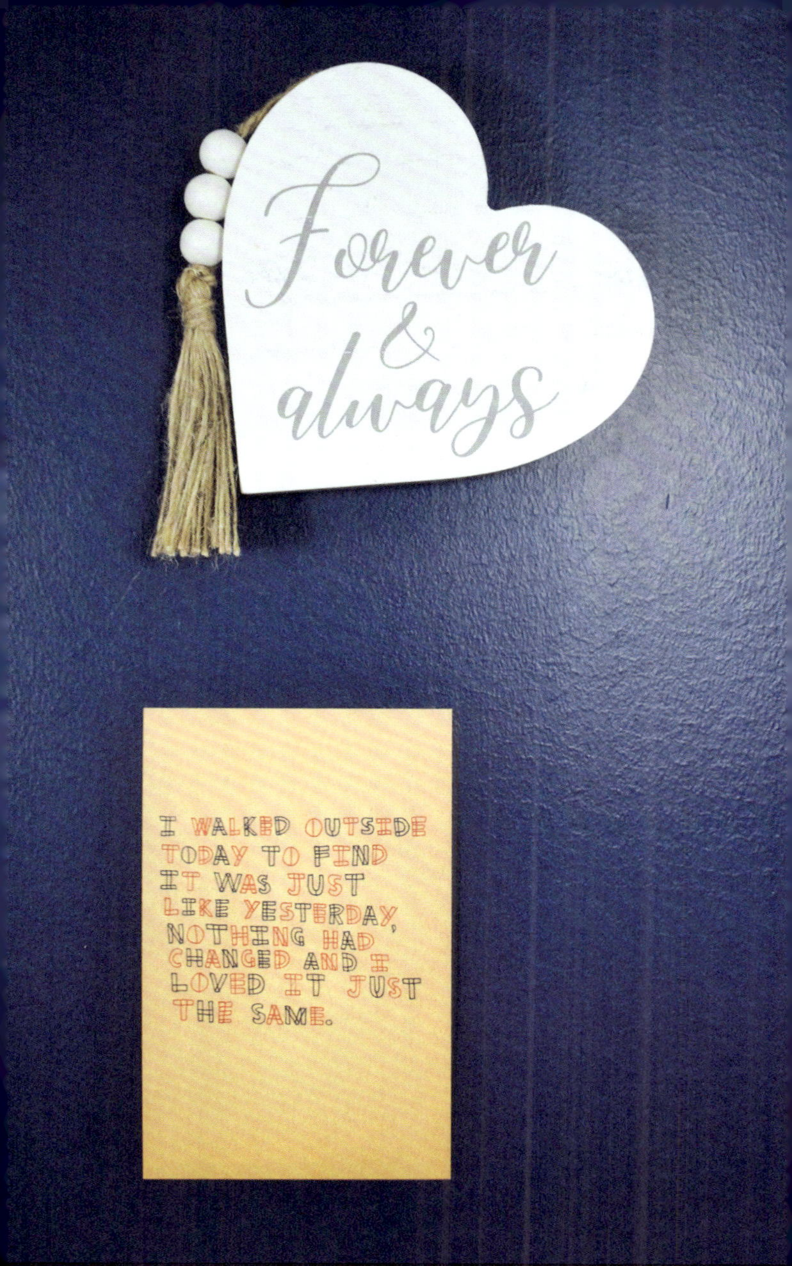
Forever
&
always
I WALKED OUTSIDE
TODAY TO FIND
IT WAS JUST
LIKE YESTERDAY,
NOTHING HAD
CHANGED AND I
LOVED IT JUST
THE SAME.

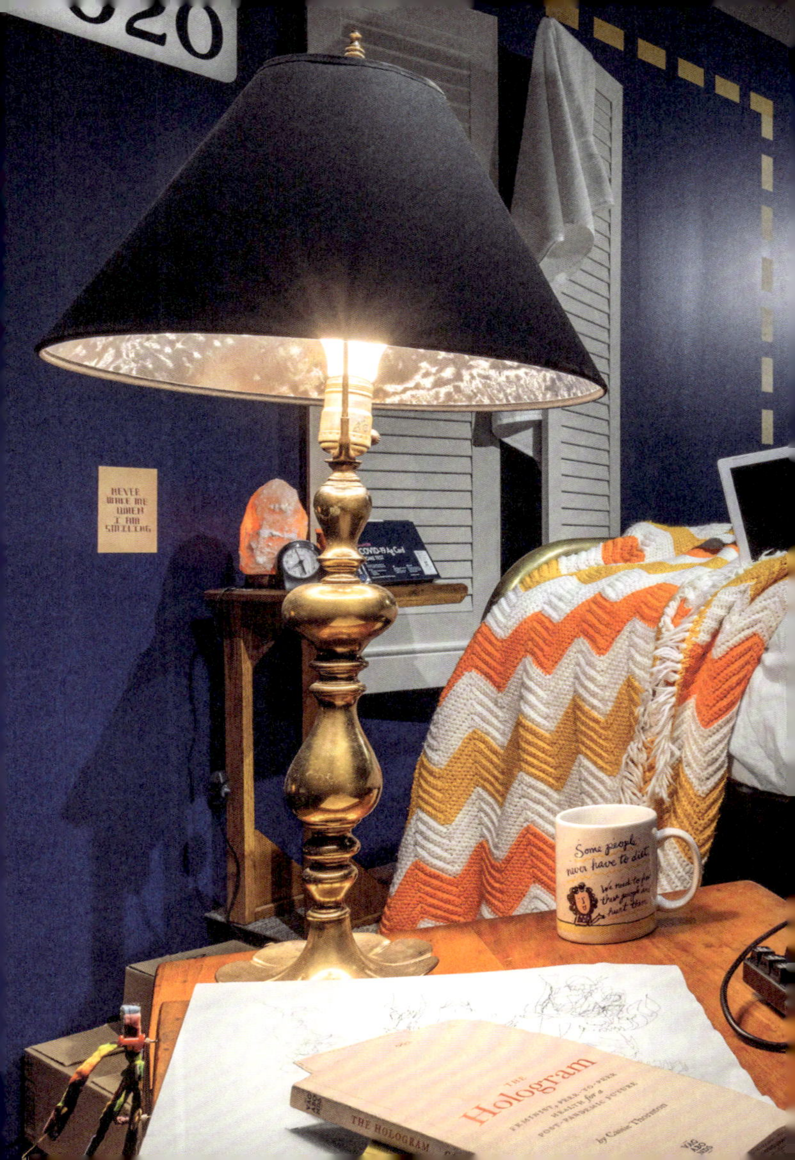
NEVER WAKE ME WHEN I AM SMILING
Some people never have to diet.
THE Hologram
FEMINIST, PEER-TO-PEER HEALTH for a POST-PANDEMIC FUTURE
by Cassie Thornton
THE HOLOGRAM

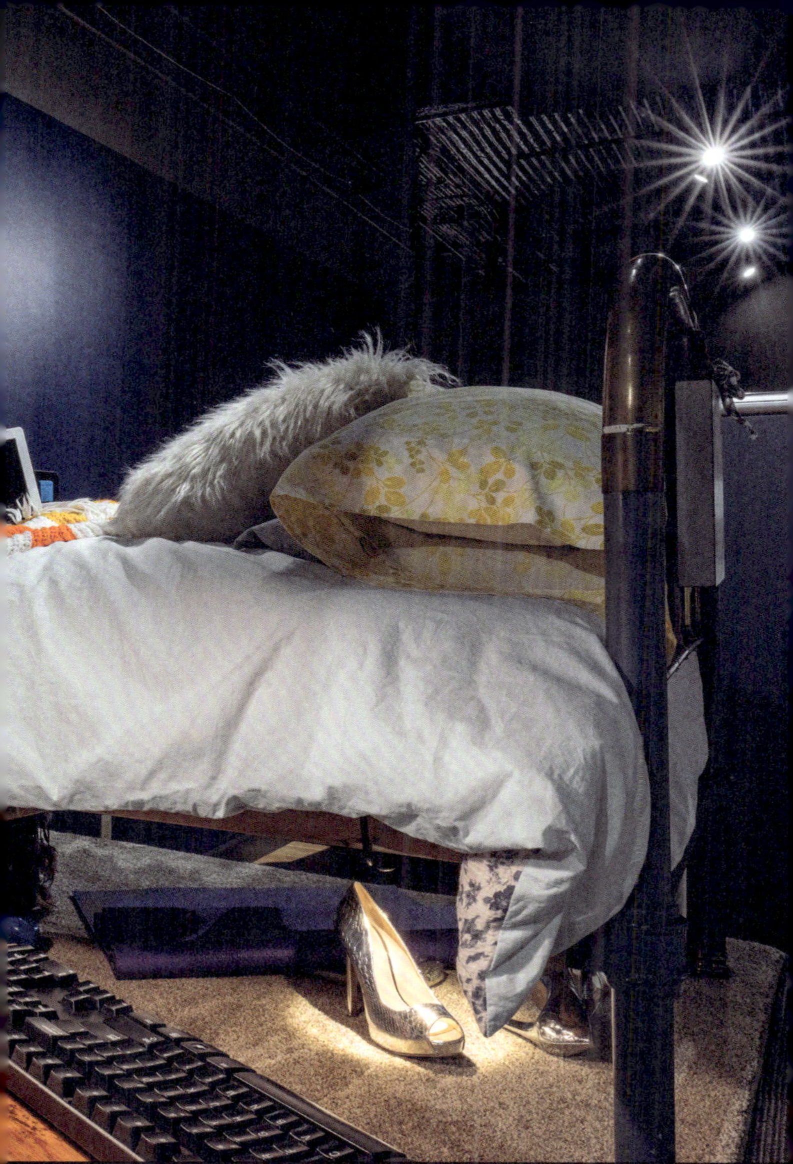

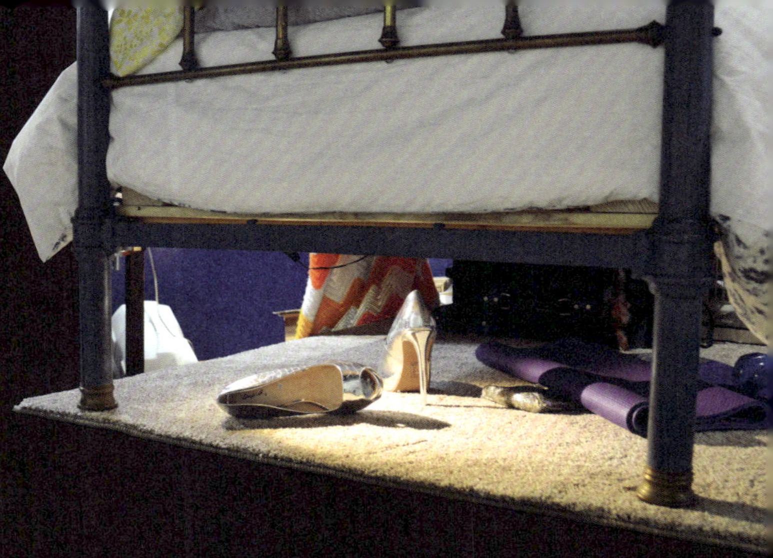

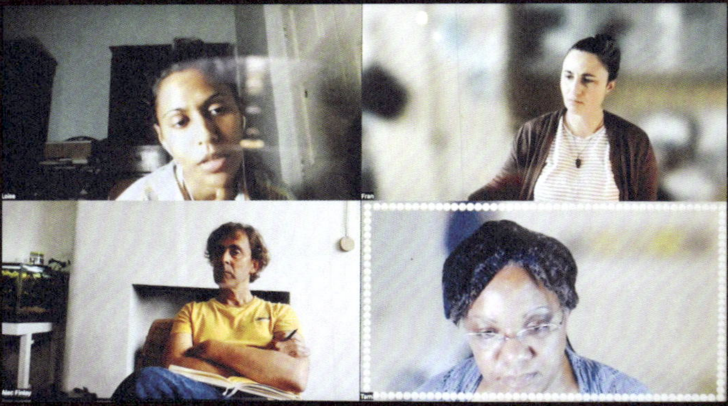

I love that the recording of my first Hologram experience was included in the exhibit. Participating gave me the tools to explain the practice to our visitors in a meaningful way. I remember feeling anxious and apprehensive about the experience but left with a real sense of peace and comfort in the end.

2038

← In The Great Isolation, many people hid things under the bed. Some of those things were costumes for outings that they could not attend, or suitcases for trips they couldn't take. But for many people, all their wishes and dreams had to be packed up and put away. It is possible that the lack of wishes and dreams present before the pandemic were part of why we got into the mess in the first place.in the first place.

← *The Hologram* is a practice that began online in The Great Isolation using corporate video chat software that spied on people and then sold the data to a violent, artificial predatory species known as "corporations." This happened via The Internet (a now-obsolete, addictive network of rudimentary computing machines largely controlled by these corporations). Thousands of people who were incredibly lonely and overwhelmed with the individual and collective crises they faced found that they could actually get energy from supporting other people, and that doing so made it easier to ask for help.

My first Hologram was the in-person workshop we held at the exhibit launch. I remember worrying about being vulnerable in front of strangers and was not expecting to develop such natural connections to them within a brief time.

What do you remember from 2020?

What kind of support do you wish you'd had?

What is impacting your life today, in 2038?

Why are you doing so well? Was it the support systems you set up during or after the pandemic?

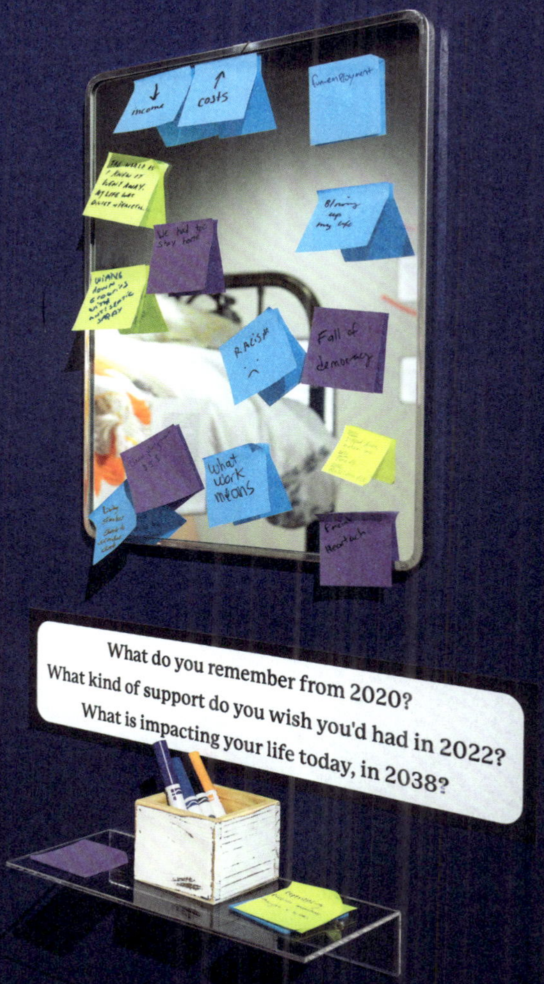
What do you remember from 2020?
What kind of support do you wish you'd had in 2022?
What is impacting your life today, in 2038?
income
costs
Blowing up my life
Fall of democracy
What work means

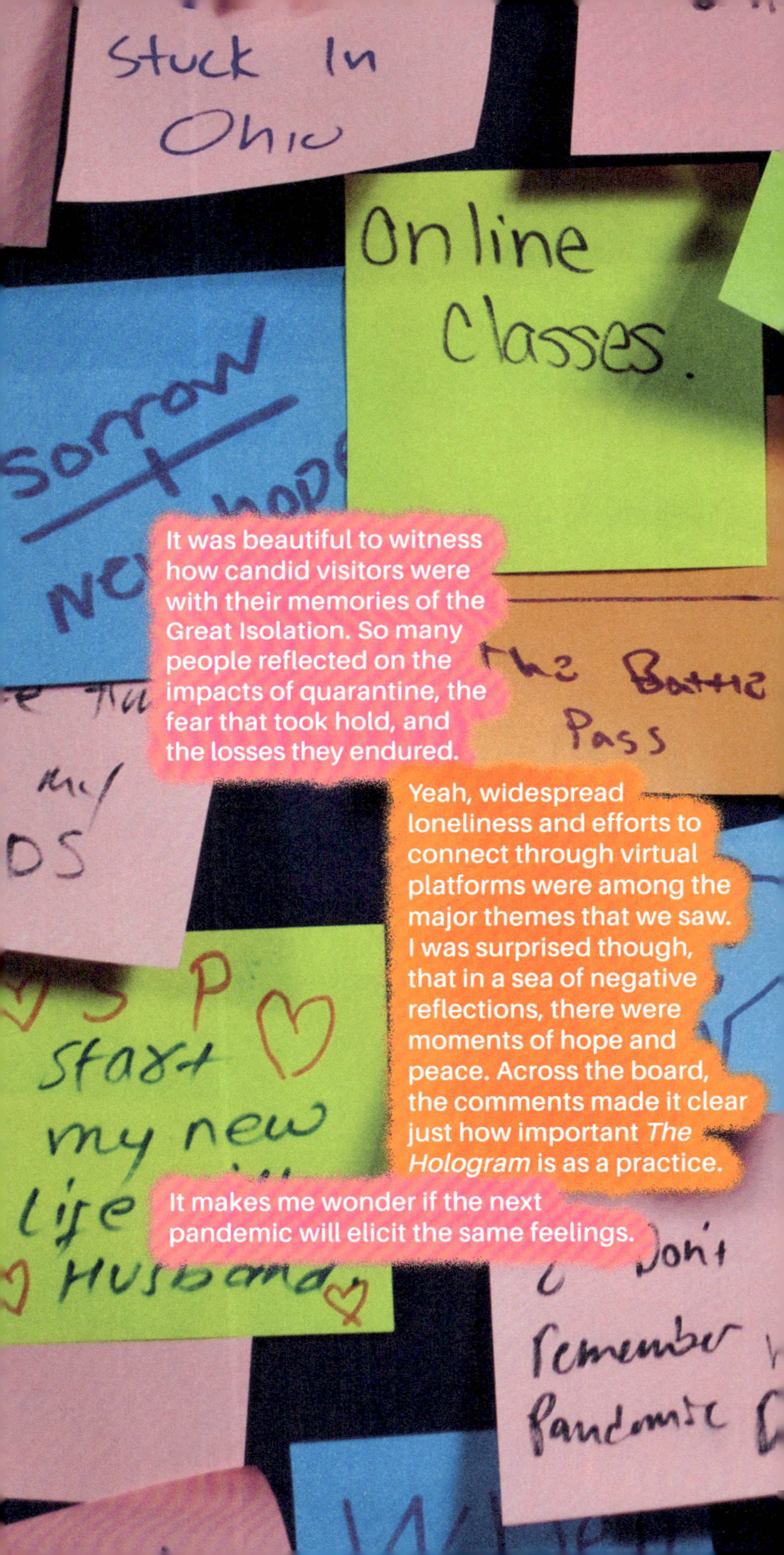

It was beautiful to witness how candid visitors were with their memories of the Great Isolation. So many people reflected on the impacts of quarantine, the fear that took hold, and the losses they endured.

Yeah, widespread loneliness and efforts to connect through virtual platforms were among the major themes that we saw. I was surprised though, that in a sea of negative reflections, there were moments of hope and peace. Across the board, the comments made it clear just how important *The Hologram* is as a practice.

It makes me wonder if the next pandemic will elicit the same feelings.

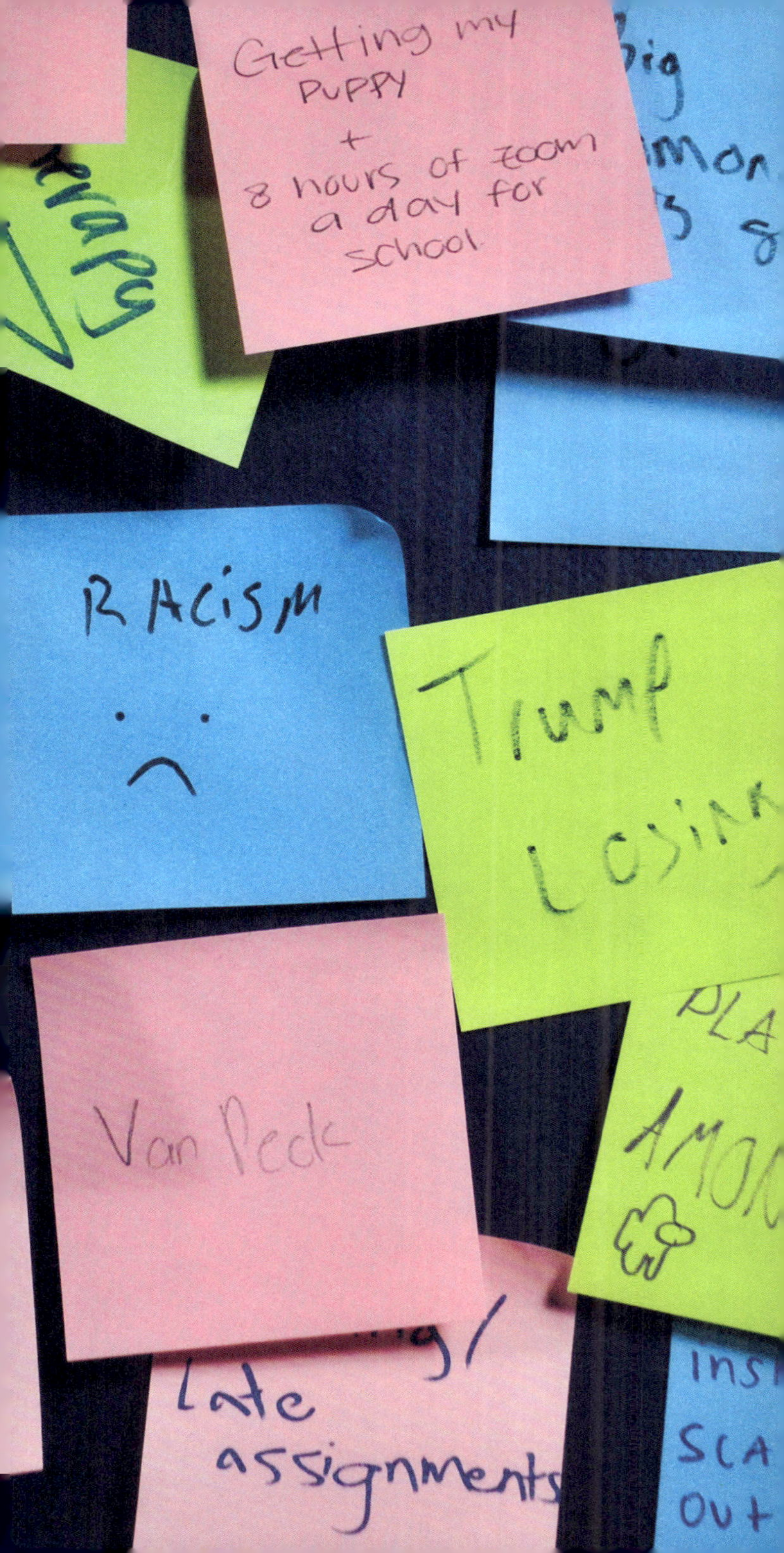
Getting my puppy + 8 hours of zoom a day for school
RACISM
Trump
Van Peck
late assignments

So, what do you think was the hardest thing to explain to our visitors?

The exhibit was just so multi-layered. There is just no quick way to explain the practice, the impact of the Great Isolation, and the development of *The Hologram* over time. The project was created by an artist but sits outside of the art world. It was exhibited in the National Museum of Psychology but wasn't the work of a psychologist. All these layers required time to explain, and I found it helpful to begin by clarifying that *The Hologram*, above all, is a social practice.

I think the visual aspect of the exhibit helped to capture a lot of those elements, though. Visitors felt connected through their own experiences of the Great Isolation which made it easier to help them understand the development of *The Hologram*.

2038

NOTES

1 Martin Placek, "Packages Delivered by Amazon Logistics in the U.S. 2018-2022," statista, published December 25, 2024, statista.com/statistics/1178979/amazon-logistics-package-volume-united-states/.

Right, but the one piece of advice I shared with each of our visitors is that you really need to try it to get it.

I could not agree more.

PREMEMBERING

Cassandra

I am writing from 2038, a year I've been obsessed with since 2020. Eighteen years ago, sitting in my little COVID-safe sublet, I received one of my first writing invitations. It came from Alina Kolar, then editor at *Arts of the Working Class*. She asked me to write an article about a new utopian infrastructure in the year 2038. I wrote about *The Hologram*, an idea that I spent a lot of time thinking about alone in my bedroom. Many people in the four years prior had told me it was cute but impossible to reorganize the way we do care using 3-D image generation as a metaphor. Before The Great Isolation, no one had time to do any more support work than they were already doing. The project was safely relegated to art, to poetry, to theory–but was categorically impossible as a world rebuilding practice.

Early in my experience of The Great Isolation, I giggled in bed as I wrote an article for Alina that was formatted like a Wikipedia entry. The article was written as if it was the year 2038, reflecting on what revolutions could happen if all caregivers were cared for by three people using the Hologram protocol. What I didn't realize then is that I would travel to 2038 to do research for an upcoming exhibition, and that 2038 would never end. In 2020 I used the writing of the Wikipedia article as a way to pre-remember (to predict a memory that could take place in the future) a moment when *The Hologram* broke out of the isolation of my individual daydreams. When it stopped being my art project and became a large social project used by people around the world. When it softly and subtly became a fundamental organizing (weaving?) method in a social world that had ruptured and needed a new way to exist. What I didn't know then that I do know now is that many things would have to break in order for this to happen, and it might start with *The Internet.*

The original Wikipedia Article is available, as it states, to all Memory of the World Members, which is everyone. Since the day when the Internet ended, January 19th of this year (2038), you have to go find a Pirate Librarian and download the article (or anything else you are looking to read) onto a clean USB. If you are in the years before 2038, the article is also still available while you are still able to access The Internet, at the *Arts of the Working Class* "website," and is called *The Hologram*. This article, in some way, gave us the conceptual formula that we used for the exhibition we've been describing here. I see this Wikipedia article as proof that the project of *The Hologram* was always meant to be used to disrupt the global economic system. It was never meant to be just art, and could never be contained in an exhibition. But we also didn't know how it would all go down.

WIKIPEDIA
The Free Post-Internet Encyclopedia

Welcome to Wikipedia,

The free post-internet encyclopedia
that anyone can edit.

Version 273.4
Last edited on ??.??.2038, at 23:19 (UTC)
Downloaded on ??.??.2038, at ??:?? (ET)
from the Pirate Archive East

Type here and press ENTER to search

The Hologram

From Wikipedia, the free post-internet encyclopedia

This article is about the Parafictional Social Practice Art Project. For other uses, see Hologram (disambiguation).

This article needs additional citations for verification. Please help improve this article by adding citations to reliable sources. Unsourced material may be challenged and removed.
Find sources: *"The Hologram"* – news · newspapers · books · scholar · JSTOR (April 2035) (Learn how and when to remove this template message)

> *This article is free to share from your local situated or traveling Pirate Librarian under Memory of the World membership which is free to all. We recommend downloading to a clean USB and sharing it with your friends. As always, download carefully, and don't accept downloads from untrusted sources!*

The Hologram is a post-economic social organizing system composted from post-secular social practices that distribute attention, value, and health to all living beings. Initiated in the lead up to the COVID-19 pandemic (also referred to as The Great Isolation of 2020), The Hologram appeared at first to be a viral art project, but soon revealed itself to be a new social technology that assembled voluntary participants into teams of four to experiment with new models of health and social care.

The Hologram is widely acknowledged[citation needed] as a social practice and storytelling strategy that helped to facilitate some vital parts of what is now known as the post-money economy (PME): an organizing method and value system that appreciates, honors and

2038

post-money economy (PME): an organizing method and value system that appreciates, honors, and shares social and environmental resources carefully, based on their ability to produce common health and life, rather than private material wealth. There is now ("now" assumes that readers are accessing this article after January 19, 2038; for other time zones before that please refer to a Google search of PME) a widespread acknowledgement[1] that the PME took place thanks to The 2038 Problem,[citation needed] the superbug, or the epochalypse,[2][3] that left all internet and computer systems unable to represent times after 03:14:07 UTC on 19 January 2038. The result of the 2038 Problem was the collapse of the lethal digital infrastructure that had been constructed by men beginning with cybernetics during and since World War II, allowing banks, war, and prisons to destroy the world systematically, but in a cute networked way.

The viral nature of *The Hologram* practice has led to the production of a mostly human fabric used for communication, information sharing, decision-making, care, and fun. This social network was not comparable to other monetized social networks of its time (examples include Facebook or Instagram), so beginning in 2024, users began to describe it as a fabric. This holographic fabric was surreptitiously woven from devalued and unwanted resources (including care, free time, curiosity, and other feminized stuffs) in the years 2016–2038, and is known to shine at night. Woven steadily, collectively, and silently without the "4-C's" of the death-driven neoliberal era (corruption, coercion, complacence, and condescension) this fabric ("network" would be the old terminology for readers from the past) was perfectly tailored for widespread activation was perfectly tailored for widespread activation at the moment of total societal collapse of the old monetizable ways, also known as The 2038 Problem.

When interviewed, hologrammers claim ignorance of the notion that this carefully woven social fabric could offer an invisible but high-functioning replacement to the old violent ways of "social" networks built atop war and logistics. Due to its viral nature, which empowers practitioners to adapt to local and collective circumstances, *The Hologram* and its derivatives have taken many thousands of forms, but almost all are marked by some or all of a suite of common features, notably the stigmatization of private property, the use of the health accumulation index, the autonomous coordination of socially necessary labor, practices of the non-transactional exchange of attention and care, and de-schooling from competition.

Holograms do not simply produce the illusion of depth but are truly three-dimensional.

Contents

Overview and history [edit]

This section needs additional citations for verification. Please help improve this article by adding citations to reliable sources. Unsourced material may be challenged and removed.
Find sources: *"The Hologram"* – news · newspapers · books · scholar · JSTOR (February 2037) (Learn how

books · scholar · JSTOR (February 2037) (Learn how and when to remove this template message)

Starting in 2020 *The Hologram* emerged as a practice and is (as of the 2037 World Practice Census) embedded in the daily life of at least 25 million people.[4] However, when one includes its many derivative forms and unofficial uses, as well as the natural spread of its social benefits, it is said to be "bigger than Beyoncé" and more accessible. [citation needed]

During The Great Isolation, when many people's daily lives transformed from the post-industrial gig work habits through the quasi-fascist healthy life strategy,[5] an artist now known simply as Cassandra initiated mostly among other precarious artists a series of small-group practices known as *The Hologram*. In Greek mythology, Cassandra is cursed to utter true prophecies but never to be believed, leading to the common rhetorical usage of the term to refer to someone issuing unbelievable warnings. (In subtle contrast, today the term refers to an accurate prophesy that cannot be believed, but must be adhered to, to forestall potential calamity.)

Since 2020, *The Hologram* practice has grown into what most experts consider to be a fundamental element of social life,[citation needed] and it is popularly believed, especially among its practitioners, to be a tendency that has always been dormant in the human experience. Most practitioners agree that *The Hologram* was originally developed by estranged artists (a now-obsolete "job" category) mostly living in jurisdictions at the heart of former capitalist and colonialist empires ("cities" that had the highest rates of suicide, addiction, and depression before The Great Isolation[citation needed]). Most origin stories colonialist empires ("cities" that had the highest rates of suicide, addiction, and depression before The Great Isolation[citation needed]). Most origin stories hold that these artists were organized by the figure named above, Cassandra, though historians have questioned her influence and even her existence.[6] Today, the practice has become a central element of the global solidarity social architecture—GSSA.

According to most practitioners and many historians, the historical figure Cassandra was an anxious and self-conscious artist who, early in 2020, released a formula for social participation in "collective health" while temporarily residing in the City of London (then the capital of a violent political formation known as a "nation-state"[citation needed] called the United Kingdom). Said to be twitchy and sweaty from having lived a socially complicated and transient life, waging an unsuccessful war against a system of exploitation known as capitalism. Lore has it she would say things like, "I wonder what a post-individualism feminist economy looks like, and if I can be trusted to imagine it?"[7] (With the violent but predictable extinguishing of The Internet some decades later [see The 2038 Problem], almost all of Cassandra's written records have been lost.) It is believed that she moved to London in the days before the outbreak of the COVID-19 pandemic in 2019. Historians surmise that *The Hologram* was meant to be something artistic and confrontational in step with the other art of the time.[citation needed]

In a passage widely credited to Cassandra, she describes the way "The Great Isolation granted the canvas needed for many people—who carried the burden of privilege like a pair of golden handcuffs attaching them to a comfortable captivity of reality attaching them to a comfortable captivity of reality avoidance—to re-draw their lives and their daily routines."[8] In what many consider to be divine providence, The Great Isolation was the time when *The Hologram* was first disseminated seriously through workshops and public events on The Internet (a now-obsolete addictive network of rudimentary computing machines largely controlled by a violent artificial predatory species known as corporations).

According to the oral history shared by most factions and tendencies that ascribe their lineage to *The Hologram*, at the height of The Great Isolation most social events and many meetings related to work and culture began to take place on The Internet including the initial Hologram workshops. People from all over the world began to correspond during weekly meetups led by Cassandra. Thanks to its viral and adaptable nature, within a year of its launch it is estimated that 250,000 people were practicing some version of *The Hologram*. Starting in around 2028, Mondays (a now-obsolete and much-hated period demarcating one full rotation of the earth within an arbitrary cycle or seven such periods developed to expedite the exploitation of labor) were designated the day of Social Holography at Home (Shh) though much folklore suggests that similar days committed to collective forms of care have been common in human social organization throughout the history of the species.

The success of *The Hologram* is often attributed to the effect of the COVID-19 pandemic and the social unrest it triggered. In the years following the pandemic, the earth lost most of its warlords, both in the sphere known as "government" and in the sphere known as "the economy" in a succession in the sphere known as "government" and in the sphere known as "the economy," in a succession of failed rocket launches, where the warlords perished seeking to escape the ecological and social destruction they had unleashed. Most historians agree that sabotage was likely a factor in some if not all explosions.[citation needed] In the vacuum left behind, the practice of *The Hologram* became ubiquitous on nearly every continent. It started as something quite humble, advertised like a pyramid scheme (a secular and populist capitalist religious practice) and discussed on morning talk shows (a daily capitalist spiritual observance). The earliest written record we have related to *The Hologram*, by an anonymous writer, speaks of it as "women's new work: a way to distribute the compulsory grief associated with the trauma of losing all the world's warlords."[citation needed] But quickly *The Hologram* morphed into a type of party line, where women, gender nonconforming, trans people, and revolutionaries of all sorts sat on couches, at home, all over the world as they discussed how good they felt about the erasure of power. The practice was used to ensure that health and stability continued as the users of *The Hologram* prepared to defend and protect the new non-hierarchy that had arrived.

In 2022 an art exhibition (a now defunct gatekept spatial ritual wherein an expensive, educational, and sometimes beautiful spectacle is created in a white room for very few as an elegant way to make sure all the people who contributed to the installation get tired and sometimes sick) by Cassandra took place at the Cummings Center for the History of Psychology. This exhibition invited viewers to pretend it was 2038 while they looked back at 2020, to understand how The Great Isolation affiliated with the COVID-19 pandemic

Great Isolation affiliated with the COVID-19 pandemic contributed to the birth of *The Hologram*. The artist made a research trip to 2038 as a way to prepare for the exhibition, and part of her never returned. During this visit she realized this was the longest year ever, because once it became 2038, we stopped counting years with numbers. No matter when you are reading this, it is still 2038 and Cassandra is there writing articles, populating Wikipedia (though The Internet no longer exists and there is no money). She finds that Wikipedia is the best medium to communicate with people across time zones, and is able to use her prophecy to work with people living in her original time zone, which (as of this update) is located about 19 years ago. Though Cassandra had predicted and written extensively about the collapse that would take place in 2038, she did not believe her own prophecy.

How it works [edit]

The Hologram is so common a part of the daily routine of the people who use it that it can be quite hard for them to define where it ends and where the rest of their life begins.[citation needed] Original instructions, which were written by Cassandra before The Internet ended, can be found in part in the Internet Archives, and are reproduced here for the sake of authenticity, and as a sample of the quaintly archaic, yet undeniably forward-looking language.

(Present-day readers are warned that, when reading this outside of the original context, they will encounter references to the individual, to private healthcare, to ownership, and to the boundaries between oneself and the other. Do not be offended healthcare, to ownership, and to the boundaries between oneself and the other. Do not be offended by these. Please remember that this was written before The Great Isolation, before the turn towards collective desires; the content was/is not intended to be offensive.)

"*The Hologram* is a simple social practice that you can organize to take care of your own health, and it will help you take care of other people at the same time. This practice does not replace going to get whatever kind of medical care you already have, want, or need. But it will help you and your community to give better care, by distributing care work between groups of people to take the burden off individuals.

Your health is multidimensional, like a hologram. Imagine if you had three people asking you about your health: someone concerned about your physical health, someone else asking you about your mental/ emotional experience, and another interested in understanding your social life? These three people would not be experts, they would be friends or acquaintances…

Invite three people who you trust to make a commitment to meet with you every season, to be a part of your Hologram. That would mean that they all would meet with you for an agreed upon time and ask you really good questions about how you are doing...

...They would help you see yourself by seeing you, in all your dimensions. They would begin to develop an alternative record about your long-term health, they would see your patterns and help you see them too, and they would help you do co-research when you need to make a big decision, or accompany you need to make a big decision, or accompany you if you need in person support at an important moment. These people are not experts...

No one wants to receive care from someone if the caretakers' needs are not being met. That is why it is important that the members of your care triangle are working towards finding three people to care for them... How can you be supportive of the people who care for you, so that they know that their own support system matters? Not just for you but for their whole community?

After you are comfortable receiving care as a hologram, the real healing begins when you extend your energy to support someone else. The most important part of this model happens now: You need to make someone else a hologram."[9]

Criticisms [edit]

Sometimes referred to as the last laugh of capitalism, no one knows if *The Hologram* is actually as pure as it seems. Elder critics with pre-Great Isolation memory have labeled it a West Coast (referring to the former North America and the land that used to be known as California) Social Practice (an art form labeled by Ted Purves in San Francisco, CA) cult. Its central organizer, Cassandra, tested positive for internalizing the values and behaviors that she learned from her cultural heritage in the US of A, where her death was her most direct way of getting enough job security to pay rent.

Magda was one of the main organizers behind *The Hologram* in 2023. When she began that work, she was a curator. The following is a transcript from a Hologram that took place on January 3, 2038 in a video chat between friends in Berlin, New York, Felixstowe, and in an unspecified location in Vermont.

Magda called her triangle to come together in 2038 to look back on her work in the art world.

2038

LIFE AFTER CURATING

Magdalena Jadwiga Härtelova, Ruth Catlow, Prem Krishnamurthy, and Amanda Nudelman

MAGDA Thank you for meeting me. Happy New Year. It's such a strange coincidence, because I just ran into Cassie outside my apartment the other day, and she looked exactly the same as she did in 2023, which was a little weird! Though I am not sure if it was a dream or not, that rendezvous reminded me that it has been about two years since we last met in a Hologram. I think I got busy and the prospect of scheduling felt a little too much. I'm so glad to be back doing our thing.

I feel like I'm a little fuzzy on the Hologram protocol. It's been a while. So maybe as we go through it, we can put it together and repeat what we are doing. I don't even remember from last time who had what role. Obviously, I'll be the hologram, the one who you ask questions to. But I can't remember who had which angle.

PREM I can't remember either. It's been two years. Maybe you can just assign us the triangle roles.

MAGDA Okay. That works. I would like Ruth to ask me questions about the social angle of my health and everything. So, if I remember correctly, that's anything from relationships, to money, to politics. And then Prem can ask me questions about my physical well-being. So that's the body, but also food, earth, and anything material. And then, Amanda, you can ask me questions from an emotional and mental angle. It doesn't have to be super clearly demarcated. If you feel like asking something else, that's totally fine. The assigned angles are just there so all the areas of my health are more or less covered.

First we do the stuck dance, and then I will tell you what I would like to focus on. Then the hologramming itself is going to start, when you can begin to ask me questions. It's okay if it feels a bit chaotic.

RUTH So for the stuck dance, this is how we do it in my Hologram: One at a time, we each bring to mind something that we're feeling stuck with in our lives. There are always things, big or small. And we allow our bodies to take a shape to express the feelings that we have around the thing we're stuck on. Then we go around and the other three take turns to describe what they've seen in the sculpture that they just witnessed. It's not interpretative analysis, it's a description of what we have seen in the body. And then we all go around making sculptures until we finally end with Magda going last, because she is the hologram.
I can go first.

[Ruth does stuck dance]

PREM Even though we were chatting before that you might do a stuck dance about your back pain and the difficulty of it, your

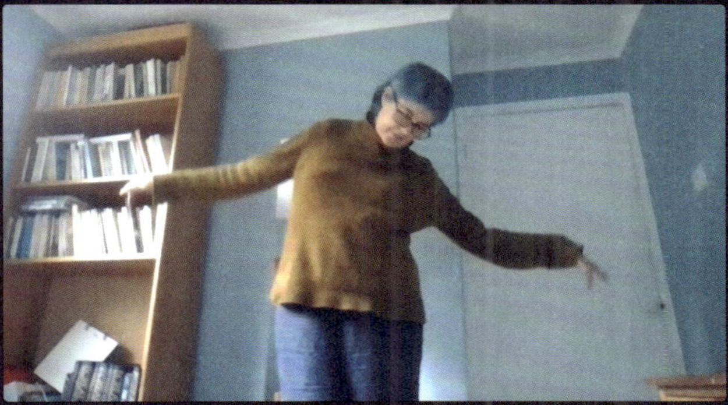

sculpture has an odd grace to it, almost a swan-like quality. The shape very much flowed from one limb to the next.

MAGDA I saw your wrists plus two points somewhere between your shoulders and neck being held on invisible strings. The rest of your body was actually very rooted and steady in one place

AMANDA I saw a kind of ferocious desire to expel something from your body by using this motion, as if you were extracting from one side and expelling through the other with quite a committed energy.

[Amanda does the stuck dance]

MAGDA I saw you being bundled, as if a straitjacket was on your arms. Your head was in a similar position as when you lay down in bed looking at your phone. There was a sense of constraint from the outside, putting your body into a rectangular shape.

PREM That's interesting because I

thought of it less as a rectangular shape and more like a cone.

RUTH I was very aware of the fact that you made a curve on your back with your shoulders by bringing your shoulders forward, and then you dropped your head down into the middle of the curve. So your head was quite protected by the curve that you made across your back.

[Prem does the stuck dance]

RUTH Something *unusual flew by, took* your attention, and held it. It wasn't shocking to *you. But it was* significant.

AMANDA I saw a kind of lengthening, physical and mental stretching, searching toward a source of something that needed attention.

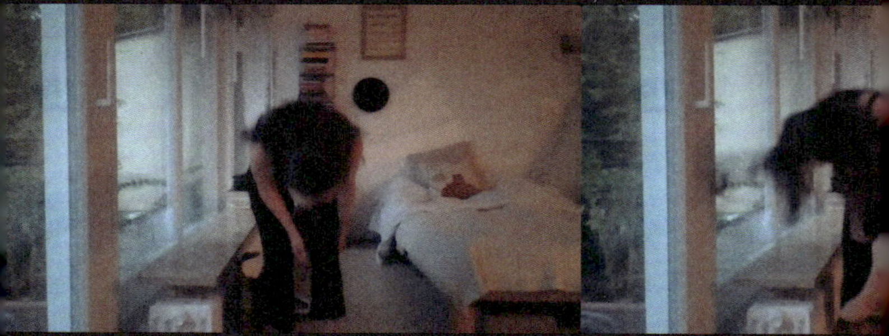

MAGDA It seemed to me very much like an exercise, because your body was very steady, rigid, and you moved just your head. In this physical exercise, you might have been looking at something you imagined, something that is not there.

[Magda does a stuck dance]

PREM It's going against gravity, trying to contort the body in a way that maybe it can't. And then the awkwardness of trying it and stumbling.

RUTH Your stuck dance was very funny because it looked like something impressive was about to happen and then you just gave up on it, and you didn't give it another go.

AMANDA Yeah, it was a way to approach something in a radically new way, trying something super different to solve a problem that is a known problem, and then a kind of joyful surrender to the fact that this is not going to be the way to solve it.

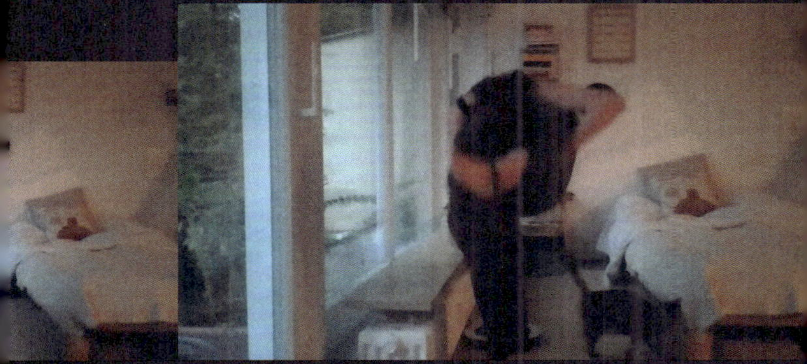

MAGDA Thank you. It's funny how much even these descriptions tell me about what I'm about to bring.

I'm gonna mark the task to start things off. As you all know I still live in Berlin, which is really surprising. I didn't think I would stay here, but as traveling got hard I got kind of stuck. I live and work in this big housing project that serves as a transition center. There are about 20 of us living here long term, plus rooms for people who need to stay short term because they are going through a transition (moving, changing living situations, personal transitions, hiding from the state, etc.). It's been a year of big storms in northern Europe. They have been even worse than the past years and so alongside my social facilitation job–thank God for UBI [universal basic income] which makes this possible!–I have also been doing a lot of maintenance on the house.

That is my general life situation. What I would like to talk about are some reflections on my curatorial past that have been affecting me lately. You all heard me talk about Kit before, this young person who I am friends with. I've been parenting and supporting them for nearly a decade now. In the past three years, my relationship with them has been a big part of my life. They're an incredible human. They're 13 now and about to move to a different house because they want to live with their other friends in a different part of the city. So we won't see each other on a daily basis. Their moving out feels like it marks the end of my early forties.

As Kit and I were packing and moving, we came across some of my old books, including the ones about curating. Looking through my catalogs from the late 2010s and early 2020s brought out such a weird mixture of feelings. As you know, I don't really curate anymore; not as I used to when I moved to the house project about 10 years ago. Back then, I still hosted a gallery in my bedroom, showing artists inventing resistance strategies in my private space. But that project slowly turned into less of a gallery and more of a social-educational center, where we teach a lot of collective health practices, including *The Hologram*, alongside many things that used to be called art. We host all kinds of workshops and services like Theatre of the Oppressed, acupuncture, massages, we offer detox support, and do what used to be called in the UK "social prescribing," meaning connecting people to infrastructures, from free food to doctors to support groups. When I was recently sitting in my room sifting through books about exhibitions on accessibility (you know, old school exhibitions with art pieces hanging on the walls in vast white empty rooms) I didn't know what to make of it, to be honest. I wonder if anybody can even imagine what it used to be like to be a curator in the old sense of the word. We did such a strange thing! Which is why I wanted to talk to you three about it because you have been there or are still connected to exhibition making.

I'm so aware of how fast life has become in some ways, especially here in Berlin at the transition house. I couldn't have imagined how marked by the seasons it would be. Between the freezing temperatures in the winter and the killing heat in the summer, and the storms in between, we just kind of hunker down and do our best to go through each crisis, to prepare for the next season.

And yet, as I was going through these books, I was grieving the past life they showed. I remembered when we could just make exhibitions for a living. At the same time, it seems very silly now: how preoccupied we were with talking about things, how obsessed we were with criticizing or finding the "right framing," instead of just doing what we talked about. Most of the catalogs were from the late 2010s, the world was already on fire back then. Together, all the feelings mixed into something that felt a lot like shame. I'm not sure that is the right description for all I felt, though, looking at the books with Kit. I would like to get to the bottom of my feelings with you. Maybe it wasn't shame, but a question of whether or not I have done enough. In the books, I saw how I spent my twenties and early thirties. And now I was sitting next to this young person who has all that life in front of them. Except Kit's life is rough in ways I couldn't have imagined. I'm asking myself: Was what we did a luxury? Is there a place where our past makes sense in this world? I find a lot of joy in the integrated arts and the social work that I do now. The feeling that I would like to create from us talking today is some sort of knowing how to be in this unknown. I never thought that by my late forties I would still be so unsure about what's meaningful in life. And so finding some sort of a grounding point would be super nice.

2038

Was what we did

a luxury?

Is there a place
where our past

makes sense in this world?

RUTH What did Kit make of your curation catalogs?

MAGDA The books seem to be curious items for them. They were interested in my nostalgia. But their world is very different from what is in the books. Partially because they have no connection to what they saw in the books. The luxury goods art market, which is the only thing that currently resembles the old school exhibitions of my early career, is so far from anything they have access to. Partially because they are 13 and at the moment they are mainly busy hanging out with friends of a similar age. Together they are setting up spaces in the cracks of the city, running a rough news and information network. They're just blooming in the chaos.

PREM In your current life, where do you get the sense of purpose or mission from? Do you feel it at all? How necessary is that for you? Is that tied up in Kit? Or is it happening in other things?

MAGDA Prem, do you remember the exhibition that Cassie Thornton did in my bedroom gallery back in 2023? There was this diagram, a graph of two lines on the window, the white upper one slowly declining, the bottom red one coming closer and closer to it in spikes until they intersected. The graph was depicting the point when the state of crises and capitalism's death ruins hits wherever you are, living your comfortable "flat white" life. Back then, I still used to imagine the lines meeting as a point.

And so I did a lot of intellectual work and some social work to prepare for the moment. Except it wasn't one point. It just slowly creeped in, we saw it happening around the world for the longest time, and then one day we realized we were already there, we were in the red zone.

In my housing project, and in my current life, there is all this everyday meaningfulness. For instance, cooking soup for everybody, taking care of people, cleaning the house. There are also bigger structural struggles such as interfacing with the German state. On the other hand,

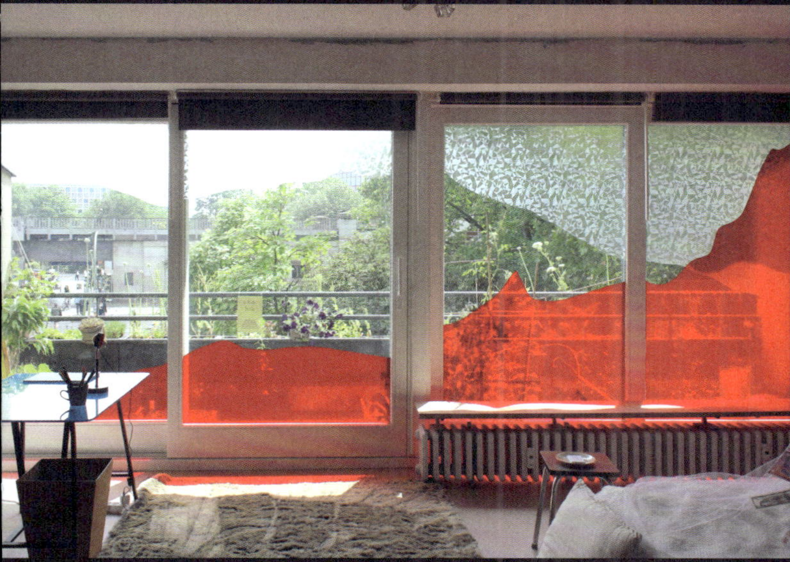

in many ways what I do in the transition house is just patching things enough so they hold, so the next storm doesn't totally flood our bathroom–metaphorically and practically.

Looking back, it seems to me that we used to be kind of trapped in abstraction. At best, we saw ourselves in preparation. Now it has hit, and I'm doing things. I feel a lot of purpose in doing. Funny thing is, though, that many of the gray zones of is-it-useful-or-not remain.

AMANDA You described that your life now feels like a series of fast-paced transitions from weather event to weather event. You have been talking about meaningfulness being when you're doing something useful. I'm just wondering if you ever make space for introspection, to reflect or grieve or feel something useless.

MAGDA I try. And funnily enough, a lot of the practices that have been born on the outskirts of the Arts are what makes spaces for such moments now. What used to be the bedroom gallery has turned into a "school" that we're running here at the transition house for sharing knowledge, exchanging skills, embodied practices. I used to speak against productivity and in favor of slowness a lot–I still would–but it's hard at times to choose introspection when we lose a friend to severe weather or the police every half a year.

There was a lot of uselessness in the arts back in the twenties, so many exhibitions churned up just to show that we were doing something, to feed the machine. It was, in a way, a relief when the divide between the luxury goods art world and the more integrated arts gaped in a way nobody could ignore anymore, when we lost the sphere of what used to be publicly funded culture. But maybe in our effort to really integrate art with real life and have it react to the current events, we have missed something, some uselessness that was very useful.

RUTH On this question of introspection, let's try to just have a moment of introspection to grow, because I feel like you resist it a little bit, like you're not sure it's allowed. Can you cast your mind back to the curatorial work that you did, that was featured in these catalogs, or of that time. What's it like? Who were the people who saw the value in your work?

MAGDA I think the goal of my work back then was the carving of occasions for people to do weird stuff. Which is something that still holds and that I try to create. There was something about the label of art that allowed people to go deep into things they might otherwise feel like they don't have the time for or that they would find too strange. I'm thinking how under the guise of participating in art, people found a lifelong support network with *The Hologram*. Or, how with the bedroom gallery I ran in the 2020s, people were always very puzzled that somebody would put up exhibitions, very thought-through complex ones, in their flat, without money or other resources. They would be nearly funnily surprised that I opened my own bedroom to strangers who found the gallery on The Internet to come and sit on my bed to watch a video, to look at art installed in my bathroom. Through which they hopefully realized that similar autonomous organizing is possible.

RUTH Looking back at that experience, what resonates most strongly with the things that are happening in your life now? What things happened then that meant that the way now could only be the way it is? What learnings came in?

MAGDA I think it is the integration of the private. The sharing of space...

RUTH What would you call that: the integration of private and...? How would you describe the blank?

MAGDA I would want to say "public," but that's not it. Maybe something like "collaborative activities."

RUTH I felt like you might want to say "philosophical." The private and the philosophical.

MAGDA Private and the discourse between strangers...

AMANDA Strangers as in "the Unknown."

MAGDA The best things I saw coming from the arts over the past decade were institutions that were brave enough to transform and change shape in really unexpected ways. There used to be a gallery called Savvy Contemporary here in Berlin. It's going to be close to ten years ago when it turned into a shelter for people without housing, but it still does retain a lot of the kind of art activities that it used to do.

We probably all know similar places that were a part of the turn into the integrated arts. But maybe with some we have lost sight of the philosophical a little bit, because the practical urgencies of our lives in between the crises can be felt so intensely.

PREM Does it have to be useful or non-useful? Maybe they're both possible... As you said, art can offer the opportunity for this encounter between two or more things that are different. So, for instance, art can function as a vector of aesthetic pleasure or joy. And bringing joy is a way of bringing liberation to an individual maker which allows them to be more responsive to other people and allows you to be more grounded and be able to encounter the world head on.

MAGDA I agree and I think it is really important that we're holding onto things that bring pleasure. The standing question for me, though, has always been the label of "art": Is it important that we built these bridges in the name of art? Looking at the books with Kit made me see again how much the chase of status and the specialness of art made us build those bridges that we were so desperately wishing for all wonky, total detours, and at times in a way that devoured whoever tried to cross them. What "Unknowns" were we actually guarding? Did our focus on laying down shining bricks make us not see what was coming? I wonder how much things are just of their own time. Was the early 2000s isolation of art from any actual working class life

Did
our
focus
on
laying
down
shining
bricks
make
us
not
see
what
was
coming?

something we had to go through? Were there things that we could have seen?

AMANDA I keep having this image of the work that you did when we were in school together, Magda, studying in the curatorial studies graduate program. You put together a presentation as part of our final symposium with an image of a cat's cradle, the string game. You're talking about feeling shame around the time that you had as a young person versus the time that Kit is having as a young person, around not being able to predict and prevent or shape it to be different. I'm thinking about what Prem said about art as a vector and how the cat's cradle is a shape with different connection points. When you put your hand in it and you pull it apart, it takes a different shape. It's all still the same thing, just a couple of strings, but now they have a different orientation to each other. I'm wondering if you can look back across that continuum, that kind of network, if you can emotionally create another way, another connection to the person that you were, that doesn't intersect through shame. Because I remember that presentation making me really feel an embodied sense of the person at the center of the curatorial work.

MAGDA I'm changing my mind. I wouldn't call what I'm feeling "shame" anymore. Looking back with you all, it feels like a time well spent. More, I would go back just for how much fun it was to curate. Curating also brought me to *The Hologram*, which then brought me to all the other social practices that

I do now. I think, more accurately than shame, I have a sense of unfulfilled potential. There was a point when many of us, in curating and the arts, felt a really strong tension between what we were talking about and what we were actually doing. We were fumbling. Especially those of us, who were doing what we called socially engaged art, which was supposed to be art whose core lay in the relationships it built. Yet, we rarely connected and bonded with each other, rarely created long-lasting relationships between curators and what we called "the Public." Over and over, we invested in things that burnt us out, we laid down our tools and said we couldn't go deeper, we opted for the immediate gratification of being visible in our bubble instead of connecting our personal lives with the struggles around us. We didn't ask each other for help much. I'm happy for my past in the art world. And I'm happy I escaped it…

RUTH Did you leave it, or did you just change it?

MAGDA Hahaha, I call it an escape to make myself feel cool. I wonder, though, if there was ever a potential for us to make a little mass movement. Do you remember how everybody talked about care in the twenties? It was everywhere in the art world at that time. I wonder if it could have turned into a movement, into some direct action.

RUTH If only we had met in 2023, it would have been crazy.

PREM I know. Can't change the past, but can change the future, I guess…

MAGDA I don't want to have us run over time and the alarm just rang. Are there any more questions?

I can describe what happens next. There's going to be two steps for closing the conversation. The first step is reflections. For which the three of you just go around and reflect on how the conversation was for you personally. If there is something that resonated with you. Something that you'll keep thinking about. Something that you really disagree with. After that, there will be time for feedback.

RUTH I have to say, all of your doubts about the value of curation made me feel so confident in the value of the curatorial, the value that all these strange philosophical practices and experiments actually brought to this time. Yes, we were all agonizing about it at the time, because of our role in extractive capitalism. But curating wasn't the only thing that was doing that. Let's face it. So, thank you. I'm so sorry it still seems to give you so much pain. But it really made me feel great.

PREM I want to second that. It made me go: *Wait, after the Cleveland Triennial, I really ditched the curator label*. But maybe I really am a curator. Maybe I don't have to call myself a recovered curator anymore. I feel reinvigorated. Also, it's great to make art. I just started yesterday, spending 15 min with the timer just doing things. I tried to teach myself how to write left-handed, because I thought that'd be fun, it made no sense. I love it. So thank you for re-invigorating my belief in art and curating.

AMANDA I have to third it because I love the idea of the integration or sharing of private and philosophical. That exploration and that kind of curiosity is the driving force. Also, you said you took all the best parts of what you learned in the mid-2010s, and the early 2020s and brought it to something that you love very much, to a person that you love very much. So your kind of professional experience that you mourn in some ways, or feel ashamed of in some ways, or have all of these doubts about is actually something that's informed something quite meaningful and precious to you. You've taken it through with you, and that feels quite meaningful. Even if the things that we were doing were totally useless.

RUTH Thanks, Amanda, for reminding me of the private plus blank, because I think that really resonates for me. That is not what the high art world is for. The high art world is for public platforms plus blank. And that is where the status comes in. You were really subverting it, essentially, finding what was under the line rather than over the line. All the stuff under that line was what you were fascinated by.

MAGDA Have I succeeded or have I failed?...

Thank you so much, everybody.

All right. Here is our last part, feedback. If I remember correctly, we devised these three ways of giving feedback in *The Hologram*, as to avoid giving advice at any moment. Since the Hologram protocol is all about just being curious. So you can choose any one of those three ways to give feedback, or all of them, or some... The first one is a wish. So: "I wish for you..." A wish can be as ambitious, as out-there, as impossible, as you would like. Nobody has to know how to get there. Second is a pattern. Maybe you observed a pattern of language or one of a way of thinking. And the last one is a provocation which is: "What if you were to do..." this and that.

RUTH Yeah, and as a seasoned hologrammer, I know that the provocation is the closest you get to giving advice... if you're really itching.

AMANDA I have a combination, because the wish is for a pattern to be revisited in a sense. When we studied together, you were coming up with your theory of curating as care. The theory was very resistant to the formal structure, the framework, you were developing it in. And you got a lot of shit for it. Yet you were very bold and just flagrant in your dismissal of what you were supposed to be doing. You emerged with this idea of caring in curating that has carried you through for decades. I wish for you to be able to revisit that kind of pattern of rebellion to the narrative that you've drawn out for yourself in terms of the framework that you live in now. This idea of usefulness, I think, could be a parallel to this idea of professionalism or historicity. And you can think about usefulness as our thesis advisor and develop some kind of a framework for rebellion against it.

PREM My wish for you is to have as much curiosity about yourself and openness as you do for Kit or with Kit. It seems like with Kit you're seeing all these possibilities, and I think you can almost think of the 47-year-old you, and I'm saying this to myself as much as I am to you to be honest, like you're just at the start of something, too. Kit is 13. You're 47. You each have this time in front of you.

RUTH I find both of those really beautiful. Mine is a provocation, which is... What if you didn't make the measure of the value of your work saving the world.

PREM Whoa!

AMANDA This is our man coming through swinging a mallet, Ruth.

MAGDA You know me too well.

You are now leaving the year 2038. You blink and you're back. If you are afraid of getting stuck in the future, you can perform the time travel ritual (page 22) backwards.

NOW

CONTRIBUTORS

CASSIE THORNTON

I'm the artist who produced the exhibition that we describe in this book. I invited everyone in this list of contributors to work on this book with me because I felt that the exhibition was worth discussing and learning from because of the way it highlighted the contradictions of being a cultural worker in the apocalypse and set the stage for questions about care and curation, theory and practice. For me, it was quite strange to work on an exhibition in Ohio while living in Berlin. I did not get to have many discussions with people about it and it felt like a parafiction (like a rumor that I told for so long that it became real) in my life. I am the person who birthed *The Hologram* and sometimes it feels like it is my child, and I am trying to give them away so they don't have to live in a fucked up nuclear family with a single mother. I think it's working. Now we have given *The Hologram* to many people around the world. I have used *The Hologram* as a practice in my life, about four to six times a year since 2020. It has made me a much more difficult person to employ because, with the stability it has afforded me, I am harder to fuck with. It has also meant that I have something to offer other people around me who I see need care and support. The nice thing is that it doesn't feel like it is all my personal responsibility to be the supporter for all my friends when they are in trouble. It feels like everyone can access care, and I can help them. I still think it is kind of hard to receive support from the people around me, but I am getting better at asking for it. When I recently broke up with my partner of eight years, I had about 10 people around me to help me get through it. It is still a struggle, but I will try to reorganize my life so I can get all the help I need without replicating old family or couple structures. I think I can do this.

For now, I don't go to doctors, just to acupuncture. I am living in Germany, though I have a US passport and residency in Canada. I am in limbo, not sure what to do about healthcare because I don't know where I want to live in the future. I am particularly worried about water. I pay for travel health insurance in Germany, and I hope to reorganize and get more long-term insurance in 2024. I am a bit worried that one day I will need some kind of healthcare treatment that is ongoing and I won't have the cash to pay for it.

As an artist I do feel like I have some small amount of power to listen and repeat back what I hear and see happening in the world. As a white cis person from the US empire, I don't always feel like I should be the person who speaks first or loudest, but I think it is within my power to know when I can and should use my work effectively to move people towards revolutionary ideas and practices. Maybe patience and precision are the powers I want to cultivate. I also feel very powerless and ashamed that I don't know how to work together with others to stop things like genocides, or how to help people who need it most. I don't feel like I have ever had free time, like

I was born with a huge list of tasks that will never be done. But recently I started experimenting with making free time and filling it with (non-art) social organizing, romance and play, and pushing the tasks away for longer and longer periods of time. This is scary, but I also feel like time opens for me when I need it, and that play and romance give me access to people and ideas that make my work happen faster and easier. When capitalism is over and there are no jobs, I will clean up the dirty burned-up planet alongside kids who I will not parent, as we learn how to be together without money, war, or schedules.

MAGDALENA JADWIGA HÄRTELOVA

I am here mainly as Cassie's collaborator. Not on the exhibition described in this book, though. I have watched the installation take form from across the ocean, while I stewarded *The Hologram* with our other collaborators.

Cassie told me about *The Hologram* right before she launched its first course in collaboration with Lita Wallis and Ruth Catlow. It was about a year and a half after we first worked together on Cassie's exhibition at the Academy of Fine Arts in Prague. At the time I first engaged with *The Hologram*, I was living in Berlin. Germany had just gone into lockdown, so everything about experimenting online with a bunch of strangers around a mutual aid protocol made the most sense, in a time when very few other things did. Cassie proposed I attend the first course and write an essay for *The Hologram* book positioning the project within the context of art, activism, and radical theory. A year later, in 2021, I was still around, now also having regular meetings with my own Hologram triangle of three people. Cassie asked me if I would want to work together on the project, to help her hold it as it was growing all its weird heads. One year later, around the time when this exhibition was taking shape, I now had a second Hologram triangle with different people. At the time of writing, organizing Hologram organizers is my full-time job.

I am quite a chronic care giver and a pretty bratty care receiver. I feel like my training in receiving care without keeping the accounts in my head is still in the beginning phases. For the past three years, for the first time in my life I have been in a network of care that doesn't feel extractive or moralistically conditional. This experience is still blowing my mind.

I'm afraid of doctors. I think they wear white coats to scare people. I think waiting rooms serve the same purpose. I do come from a country that has "free" public healthcare, a remnant of its socialist past, and I have lived most of my life in places where this is the case. I'm currently getting into financial debt because the health insurance required in Germany is too high for me to cover with my freelancing. Is this better than living without it?

When I studied curating in San Francisco, the very first day of our program, our teachers organized a little get-together of the newcomers with the second years and the teachers, a mixer. In the middle of it, the head of my program, the late Leigh Markopoulos, got a phone call from one of the second years. She was on her way to the school on her bike when she got hit by a car at an intersection. She was calling Leigh lying on a sidewalk where the passersby had moved her. She had no health insurance and had to beg people to not call an ambulance. Leigh left to give her a lift to the hospital. She was cool like that. These are all the things I know about healthcare.

ELEONORA TONIOLO

I'm the person who designed this book. I'm an active member of *The Hologram* community, facilitating Minimum Viable Holograms in person and online and showing up to weekly gatherings in Berlin. I first got in contact with Cassie after reading *The Hologram*: The book gave me a rush of hope, a sense of relief (someone that understands! and practices!), and an instinct to drop whatever I was doing to just go join a Hologram militia. What was I doing in a design master's at an institution that functions by the same logics of individualism and competition that I felt so compelled to refuse? After a generous online conversation with Magda, I joined online Community of Practice meetings and tried out *The Hologram* with strangers. I did not drop out of my master's, but I moved back to Berlin afterwards and started getting involved with *The Hologram* as soon as I could. I have a Hologram of my own, but we managed to meet only once. I've hologrammed more with "strangers" from the community than with my original triangle. The ability to care for others has always been a part of my personality. Be it because I'm socialized as a woman, or because it can provide a sense of power and control, supporting others is a rewarding activity. It's also been my experience that what goes around comes around, even if I don't think it's necessarily a universal rule. I often receive a lot of care without asking and I am so surprised every time: What did I even do to deserve it? Receiving is tougher than giving; it can be beautiful and at the same time uneasy and disorienting. If I'm needing care and help, it probably means I've lost control over an aspect of my life. Maybe getting better at asking and describing specific needs will wrestle back some of the control that would make it more comfortable.

I work as a freelance designer and I pay for healthcare in Germany. I go to doctors for my yearly checkups–I'm glad I can. Yet I'm often pissed before an appointment (because it requires dedication to get one). I'm often pissed at doctors during an appointment (because they're not able to take the time to listen and they seem to withhold information). I'm often pissed after an appointment (because I had to pay extra for those considered-extra checks that I think are basic while I didn't get to ask all the questions I wished I had asked). I also regularly receive unsolicited "natural" medicine advice and supplements from my parents. Which is fine most of the time, but I wish they'd only do it when I ask for it, because I don't trust every new miracle remedy as they seem to do. As a freelancer with poor self-promoting abilities, I have more free time than the average worker. This allows me to participate in *The Hologram*, to be part of a collective that runs a non-commercial event space on a volunteer basis, to babysit a friend's child. The type of design skills I'm fluent in right now won't help much (before or) after the apocalypse. If and when only a burned-up planet is left, and I am among those who survived, I want to help build shelters out of what's left and be available to listen and to help set up Holograms. Then, like now, I want everyone to develop emotional literacy and feel supported.

LITA WALLIS

I am into creating spaces to work our way out of the unhealthy systems we've inherited. That can look like youth work, participatory action research, or going for walks in the moss.
In the spring of 2020 Cassie asked for my help to turn the concept of *The Hologram* into a series of workshops. We wanted to create a course where we too could find out what exactly *The Hologram* was and how it worked, alongside the participants.

My other role was to help make it culturally appropriate for (more cynical, sarcastic, NHS-raised) British people like me, as we thought our first participants would be people at Furtherfield Gallery in London. But in the end, the pandemic moved the course online and suddenly we had 31 people tuning in from all over the world to help us practice and hone the Hologram protocol together, from our various different corners and cultures of lockdown.

In that course, and with the guidance of the participants, learned what "a triangle" is, why we have to start with a "stuck dance," how "we" pronouns change our brains, and why it works to end with specific forms of "feedback." Since then I've been a part of six courses, and each of them were both a place to share the Hologram tool, but also a process of collectively unlearning a different aspect of the shit capitalism puts in our heads.

Maybe it's because I am a Virgo or maybe because my brain is a chaos-monkey but I have to write notes constantly. Some of the offerings in this book are based on notes I wrote as the Hologram protocol crystalized over the years, and we started to really understand how and why it works.

Nowadays I live and work at a critical learning center in mid-Wales. I am still a hologram and in two triangles. I don't hate doctors because I was raised by one, but I think finding a good one who has enough time and continuity to truly care for you is increasingly impossible… therefore I love prescribing *The Hologram* to loved ones who have needs for care that they do not know how to meet. It continues to be a great honour to learn about myself and the world through this prism of deeply listening to other people's stuckness.

PREM KRISHNAMURTHY

I first encountered *The Hologram* during the COVID-19 pandemic, when I read a tall, narrow book outlining its core ideas. As I often do with books and ideas that I find compelling, I began to share this widely with everybody who would listen (and some who wouldn't). By the time the pandemic seemed to be improving, I had already drunk the Hologram Kool-Aid, having invited Cassie to speak in a university lecture series and having myself participated in an online Hologram workshop. Although it was late in the game, I convinced the triennial I was artistic-directing to include a Hologram intervention within the National Museum of Psychology in Akron, where I always thought it belonged. I made the project work within the budget, but since this was a triennial (and one that eventually shut down, anyways), there was not truly adequate institutional support or visibility for the project–but luckily Cassie pulled off an incredible installation. Owing in large part to the stress of the project, I lost my own mind after opening the show–an irony of ironies, since the show was focused on art as an agent of transformation, a mode of healing, and a therapeutic process. At that point, I probably could have used my own Hologram, but luckily, I had family and friends (plus German insurance and some US mental health professionals alongside several besties who also happen to be clinical practitioners) who nursed me through my recovery. Sometime later, Cassie asked me to be part of the book in your hands as part of an interview from the future. Since it's from the future, I don't have many feelings about it, or even remember it yet! But, being a generally emotional human, I'm pretty sure those will arrive soon enough.

RUTH CATLOW

I had the good fortune to be present at the early formation of the Hologram peer-to-peer healthcare system. In the spring of 2020, at

Furtherfield (where I am co-director), we hosted a series of workshops devised and facilitated by two witches: artist and debt activist, Cassie Thornton, and a youth worker, Lita Wallis. The work was resourced through the EU-funded CreaTures research project into the transformative power of creative practices for sustainability. COVID-19 wrecked our plans to work together in the flesh, at Furtherfield Commons in Finsbury Park in London. It also created an urgent need for the kind of new networks of care being created within *The Hologram*, so the workshop series moved online.

Since then, I have been an enthusiastic fellow traveler, participant, and sometime co-deviser in the practice of Social Holography. I was the first guinea pig for the Minimum Viable Hologram (MVH) in December 2020, and since then I have been supported by my own triangle of elders every couple of months. I continue to facilitate many other people to set up their own triangles. In 2021 I went deep into role for the Live Action Role Play (LARP), *We were made for this // 2050 Fugitive Planning*, in which we used sci-fi to conjure new rituals for traveling together through time, and a vision for the future transformative power of *The Hologram*. The principles of Social Holography are now woven into many dimensions of my life. As a result, I now know that asking for what I need is a very hard and extremely important practice. Also, refusing reciprocation or payment for care is a powerful way to fight capitalism and to build other worlds. The text called "Life After Curating" is based on a transcript from when I was a triangle member for *The Hologram*'s administrix, Magda, in a LARP that interrogated the value of her work as curator. We visited a world 15 years in the future (2038), weirded by advanced technologies, pandemics, and persistently uneven distributions of injustice. We asked questions from physical, mental/emotional, and social perspectives and together we generated a whirlpool of generative questions and were all surprised at the end to discover our shared, wholehearted belief in the revolutionary, life-giving properties of (at least Magda's) curatorial work. On a personal level it was productively uncomfortable to experiment with being a septuagenarian and to imagine myself comfortable with receiving daily physically intimate healthcare from a network of peers. Me and my family get our healthcare through hearty Social Holography and a national health service, still free at the point of delivery. The NHS is magnificent and has repeatedly saved our lives without bankrupting us. It is also desperately beleaguered as a result of decades of political vandalism.

AMANDA NUDELMAN

I am one of the triangle members in Magda's Hologram in 2038. I have known the person who birthed *The Hologram* (Cassie) and a person who has helped foster it (Magda) since 2015 when I met them both in the Bay Area through California College of the Arts. While I haven't yet had the opportunity to participate in a Hologram, I have followed the development of the concept/practice/invitation from afar since its inception. I have carried *The Hologram* with me as a philosophy or reminder or mantra of sorts for how powerful the human imagination can be. How radical forms of care, support, and intimacy are possible even when it feels unlikely for them to be there. I have played the role of caregiver for as long as I can remember: I was socialized as an eldest daughter in a blended family and have, for most of my life, leaned very much into all the expectations that come with that role. However, as I've gotten older, I have tried to establish better boundaries and to be more intentional with how I give and receive care. That mostly means learning to accept that settling into a space of emotional discomfort is an act of care, as empathetic connection asks us to do. My father is a physician, so I have always had an extremely privileged relationship to professional Western medicine. I usually call my dad first whenever I have a medical issue that needs attention, which he can often address without me needing to visit a clinic or hospital. I find it shockingly difficult and exorbitantly expensive (although perhaps I shouldn't be surprised after all these years) to find clinical mental health support for my depression. I am currently unemployed/an independent curator as I was recently laid off from my full-time job when the non-profit organization I worked for closed. It's weird to me that the only times in our lives in the US that we get to opt out of capitalism for a little while, with some social financial support, are under duress–without a job or on medical leave. I took on an incredible amount of debt to get a master's degree so that I could be "qualified" to do my work, so even though I'm working less day-to-day, I feel crushing pressure to return to work full-time at a non-profit as quickly as possible so I can continue working toward loan forgiveness. On good days, I feel extremely lucky to participate in capitalism the way I do, building relationships with brilliant creative people who illuminate my life and the world with art and ideas and sometimes change. This part feels very special and a little bit like cheating within the confines of capitalism. Other days I feel like I don't have very many choices about how to make my life. I can't tell if I have any free time because I'm so tired all the time. But I do go for walks with my dog, occasionally eat saag paneer with friends, drink coffee in bed with my partner, and paint watercolor portraits of the giant squirrel king who terrorizes my yard. These things feel good and I'm trying to figure out how to make them feel like more of my Life than my job(s). I hope the heart of my work won't be so different when capitalism finally implodes and the world is all used up–survival is a creative act after all.

FRAN UGALDE

I am a maker and arranger of visual, conceptual, and informational elements. As a painter and arts administrator, I truly thrive when developing systems of organization and envisioning and configuring things in space–even more so when pushing against conceptual parameters and the confines of financial, spatial, and other earthly limitations. It may be possible that aside from curating, developing, and installing exhibitions at the Institute for Human Science and Culture, my most impressive skill is to save and reuse any and every piece of material that may still serve a purpose in the future, thus saving the environment from unnecessary refuse AND maximizing an already small institutional budget. To this effect, I worked with Cassie to conceptualize *The Hologram* into the physical space of the National Museum of Psychology by offering to use old museum platforms, re-used pieces of lumber, my childhood bedframe, my yoga mat and suitcase, my mother's sewing machine and puzzles; as well as my graphic design skills, and multiple swimming trips for–very necessary–cool-downs during the hot summer exhibition preparation days.

JENNIFER BAZAR

I am a storyteller who is often "lost" in history. My work has centered around the challenge of unpacking complicated and convoluted concepts for public consumption. I am fascinated with the power of words, and the challenge of identifying intuitive connections between content and audience. As a researcher and public historian at the Center for the History of Psychology, my work takes me into the history of mental health care where I aim to share untold stories of voices silenced by those in power. This background influenced my approach to the collaborative narrative development of *The Hologram* exhibition at the National Museum of Psychology, helping both to bridge the content with the existing Museum narrative and take on the challenge of explaining the social practice of *The Hologram* in a manner that was easily absorbable by visitors.

HEATHER (HEY THERE) KAPPLOW

I am an artist and language worker based on the eastern coast of the US, but working internationally. I met Cassie in NYC in 2013 when I acted as a poetry-writing security guard in a project called Poets' Security Force that she was doing at that time at The Elizabeth Foundation for the Arts. I have been following the evolution of The Feminist Economics Department since and had a crush on *The Hologram* from afar, but sometimes I need to see and feel a thing in action/in person to wrap my brain around it. While at a residency in Berlin in 2023, I finally visited some Hologram gatherings and tried my hand at being in a few triangles. I want to go deeper, and hope to get a Hologram community started in Boston, where I currently live, as soon as my life conditions next permit it. The communities I am part of here sorely need something Hologram-like to build hope, trust, and solidarity and to help us extract ourselves from the toxic impacts of the pervasive institutional culture of this place. I live in Boston–a terrible place for me to live from a professional perspective, whatever that means–in a large part because living here gives me access to good quality state health insurance. I reconnected with Cassie in Berlin when we attended an amazing workshop on grandmothers together (led by Jamila Al-Yousef), and then felt very lucky to be invited into this project as a developmental/line editor. This meant immersing myself in the text—swimming in it over and over again—and then emerging from it and having surreal/inspiring conversations with Cassie, and eventually Cassandra, where time got weird and wobbly and magical *and now I, we, and the book itself* live on *multiple* timelines simultaneously and at least one of us has transformed into a grandmother. I hope to stay entangled with all of the efforts described by others in this contributor list. And I too worry about water...

THICK PRESS

Thick Press, a collaboration between two old friends, a social worker (Erin Segal) and a graphic designer (Julie Cho), publishes unusual books about care work and the work of care. We met Cassie at the Miss Read Berlin Art Book Fair in 2022, and later invited her to contribute to our 2024 *An Encyclopedia of Radical Helping*. (She then introduced us to many wonderful future *Encyclopedia* contributors, including Ruth Catlow.) Thick Press doesn't typically take on projects that are in their adolescence (we prefer to work on a book from beginning to end) but we decided to make an exception in this case because, for both of us, *The Hologram* resonates so resonantly, even though neither of us has ever tried it. As mothers, wives, daughters, and workers, the two of us live more atomistically than Cassie, Magda, and some of their comrades—and so it's been a joy to absorb some of their collectivist magic.

MEMORY OF THE WORLD LIBRARY

Memory of the World is a network of interconnected shadow libraries, each maintained locally and independently from the others. It is modeled after the concept of the public library, extended to the digital realm: With books ready to be shared, meticulously cataloged, everyone is a librarian. When everyone is a librarian, library is everywhere.

Public Library/Memory of the World was initiated in 2012 upon the invitation of Kiberpipa to curate their biannual HAIP festival in Ljubljana. Conceived at a moment where public libraries came under threat of austerity measures and where the networked infrastructures of sharing came under an increased threat of closing, it was aimed at strengthening and connecting those infrastructures and provoking debates that addressed the imposed and implicit territorial, socioeconomic, and legal barriers to the universal access to knowledge.

CASSANDRA (mythic)

Cassandra was a mortal in stories from ancient Greece. She was the daughter of Priam and Hecuba, king and queen of Troy. The god Apollo, enamored of her, granted her the power of prophecy but, when she rejected him, sabotaged that power with a curse that no one would believe her predictions. In modern usage, her name is employed as a rhetorical device to indicate a person whose accurate prophecies, generally of impending disaster, are not believed. She now lives in the year 2038 and communicates through Wikipedia, from where she generates content about the future and describes it for the public. For this project she contributed the Wikipedia article and The 2038 Problem. Her health is based on the comprehensive health of all people who know the future but who have been told by someone powerful that they are crazy.

PROMISES OR I'M WILLING TO STOP, TO GO BACK, TO MOVE SIDEWAYS, TO NOT DELIVER

Magdalena Jadwiga Härtelova

Back in 2017, I looked two men in the eyes at my graduate school exit interview. I promised I would never curate a biennial. "But if somebody offered you the opportunity to curate a biennial, of course you would do it! What an opportunity! You are an idealist, just think of what you could do with that kind of public exposure."

In the final semester of my curatorial practice graduate program, I wrote an essay for a class that focused on biennials. The point I was making was quite simple: I couldn't see how the biennial format–a grand exhibition allegedly presenting the best and freshest contemporary artists coming together in one location–could be emancipated in a way that would cut off its colonial roots (the ones that sprung art into a contest for contemporary VIP selection). How could any of these temporary spectacles that cost monumental resources possibly be in service of something other than elite knowhow, luxury tourism, and the unhinged free art market? Back in my graduation year, my argument was mostly built on principle. I believed, as I somewhat still do, that formats carry their original ideas with them. The Venice Biennial started as a big jerk-off circle of Western European nation-states. Therefore, I concluded, we should stop putting our energy and resources into these brand-making machines, if we're going to claim any attempt at social transformation. Abolish biennials, build something better suited to facilitating international art connections, if building that network is your goal. My professors thought the essay was a funny thought exercise. I thought it was funny too, but not in the same way. I was dead serious about my conclusion.

My promise to my professors has become one of the life-long experiments I am running on myself. I assume it won't be very hard to keep. I don't expect to be asked to curate a biennial any time soon. You see, I would love to say that my proclamation started a hard but epic ride down a publicly-acclaimed, revolutionary curatorial path. But that's not how it has felt most of the time. Mostly, I have been fumbling and stumbling and doubting myself. I have also become braver and much less employable. The art world, like academia, is very much a snake eating its own tail. If you decide that you won't allow yourself to be eaten and you step out, you stop being taken into account. That's the end of it.

One of the hardest things for me to let go of was my quest for public "justice." I had to recognize that working on actual change towards just conditions would most likely not involve my giving fiery speeches at high profile conferences or contributing to well-paid commissions from Verso's newest anthology on transformative curating. After all, that would just feed the snake. The last revenge fantasy I keep entertaining when I want to make myself laugh in the bath is imagining an invitation to deliver the commencement speech at my graduate university.

Over dinner, I would confess that I do love curating and art. Many truly radical things (and by radical, I mean "thorough and comprehensive,"[1] as Leanne Betasamosake Simpson defines this word in *As We Have Always Done*) have been happening under the umbrella of arts: the smashing of debt, abortion aid, the planting of forests to become libraries for the generations to come, zines that help people apply for discounted health insurance, community time economies, archives of the future of climate change, interspecies assemblies for park use re-negotiation, etc., etc. I have no doubt that art has the potential to spark, carry, aid in, and swell into real-life transformation. And, I have also been very angry at art for a long time. The arts is a special, though not in any way unique, nest of egoism, individualism, and exploitation, where slick words hide ugly truths about how much real-world suffering we must disregard to maintain the nest of delusions it protects. The arts is a place where we gather together over wine to pretend that we are creating a community of resistance by launching the newest digital coin. The art world is a place of violent power trips. It is an infrastructure that is meant to leave everybody worse off–that is, apart from the few dudes on top. And so, for a long time, I have had one foot in, one foot out.

Here are three stories from 2023:

✦ 1 ✦

I have been a part of such a process of stepping away from the “Big Bad Known” while working on *The Hologram*. In the public eye, the project originated in the art world. Cassie’s residency at Furtherfield and her collaboration with its curator, Ruth Catlow, catapulted the protocol into a large-scale experiment. Plus, Cassie’s speaker fees from art and academic events funded the first year of the project. But as you have read, an art experiment was never the dream behind *The Hologram*. From the beginning, the wish was for people from all sorts of backgrounds and walks of life to practice and adapt the protocol. So we could learn from each other. So the project could have a life that neither Cassie nor I could ever imagine. So that one day, this practice of intense curiosity and autonomous life-long support would become a nearly mundane part of many people’s lives. It felt like an absolute victory when our Hologram courses filled up with healthcare workers, activists, and literally, our moms. We had made it! We were in connection with inspiring people and initiatives working on real-life change. We had total strangers from all over the world getting in touch with us. In its first four years, the network became incredibly alive and expanded into the most exciting places. That’s why it was such an odd feeling when I encountered art world acquaintances who were surprised that the project was still going on. They thought we had moved onto something new because they hadn't seen anything about *The Hologram* posted on their favorite art channels in a while...

✦ 2 ✦

In a near parallel to my involvement with *The Hologram*, from 2020 on I have done most of my "traditional" curating in my bedroom. What I'm saying is that I run a gallery in my bedroom. On Tuesdays from 3:00 p.m. to 5:00 p.m. This project was bubbling in my head for a while, naturally coming alive during the pandemic. For years, I've been trying to figure out ways to combat the oppressive white-walled "professionalism" of the art institutions I've operated within–their unmovable inhuman timelines, lifeless silence, and work-for-exposure pipelines. So, that's how I ended up in my bedroom.

In 2023, in my bedroom gallery I curated a different exhibition by Cassie, this one called *Mythical Celestial Bodies*. The exhibition was about what it means to be comfortably surviving and drinking coffee during the apocalypse. At the opening, one of the first people who came was very obviously going through the initial awkwardness I've seen many people show upon entering my bedroom. They walked around a little bit, some of the performers talked to them, but as the room started filling up, they escaped onto the outdoor walkway that led to the apartment. It was clearly an undertaking for them to be in a private space filled with strangers. I can very much relate. As they were taking a breath, another person approached to check in on them. They struck up a conversation and eventually came back in to see the performance. They ended up comfortably snuggled into a corner for the opening, staying for the whole thing. They served themselves from the dinner that's always ready in the kitchen and hung out with us afterward for drinks on the lawn in front of the building. Before they left, they came up to me to reflect on what a special experience it had been. They told me what happened, how unique it felt to be seen and supported, how their perception of art changed in this setting. They will be back for sure, they said. What a special place! I would hear this often from a regular stream of strangers coming through. They would marvel on the immediacy of the space, on being able to have moving personal encounters. Yet, I have to say, they rarely followed up on their heartfelt promises of "for sure" coming back.

✦ 3 ✦

This dance of intimacy and intimidation was nearly opposite to what I observed in institutional galleries of that time. I have a couple of friends who worked for a well-known gallery here in Berlin. It's a huge space located right off one of the main Kreuzberg streets. Its street-facing wall is all windows for prime public exposure. The space has high ceilings, a professional sound system, and just a few art objects emphasized by a vast white empty space. (This gallery can serve as a placeholder for any well-funded art space of the time that prides itself on being merit-based, sprinkled with surface level "diversity.") A friend told me, and I have seen it, that it is very hard at the exhibition opening to close the event, "not even because we served free wine, but because people just hang around waiting for something to happen." Most events there consist of at least a two-hour conversation between the current artist and a guest critic, during which you had to hold your pee as long as you could because everybody frowned if you tried to get up from your chair. Plus, there are at most 20 people in the whole gallery, so it feels kind of embarrassing to walk across the vast space to the back bathrooms. After 40 minutes of painful Q&A, "everybody rushed to the bar," my friend said. "There is always the artist with their friends, having a good time. The curator was with them or in their own little circle. And then there are the rest of the visitors. You can see them walking around, they want to meet someone important, they scout for an encounter. They think something might happen to further their career but it never does. They want to tell someone what they think. They hang out on the side until we have to kick them out. For them, I wish they would just go to a club."

✦

What I'm trying to say is that the art world seems strangely stuck between wanting connection but not knowing how to go about getting it. Like a child who has been taught that "care" equals dominance and that vulnerability is a sure way to hurt and ridicule. We built up a lot of walls, material and social, to protect our egos. When will we notice that inside of them we are all miserable?

When I dream of 2038, I wonder if our current torn attention and priorities are all part of a collective stuck dance we need to do before we change. Here, now, in my thirties, I have been lucky enough to know that another world is possible, to have experienced art that is fully integrated in everyday life. Still, I am so very unsure if I will make it to a version of the future where my heart is leading me, if I will be able to work in the unknowns and withstand the pressures. Is it our fear of discomfort that has held up the art world for so long? Are we scared–and is that why we go back to the hyper-corporate, slick aesthetic art spaces? Or did we get overwhelmed imagining something–anything–different? Out of pure habit, are we latching onto the ideas of beautiful, cold sense-making? I have my hopes but I'm not sure: Are we just about to break into an-other world or are we having a party in a dead alley?

Luckily, we make the future as we go. As long as we are willing to admit a mistake and back out of dead alleys, we are okay *We will need* an inordinate amount of thoroughness to navigate through the changes *and challenges* that are coming. We will have to get real artistic to figure out an honest life on a planet we set on fire, to protect each other from becoming chewed up by AI-operated logistics that will, soon enough, determine where we can move, how we work, and whether we are useful. Along the way, making some promises might be useful, so we remember where we're heading. Here is a renewal of mine: I won't let people exploit my attention for their promotion anymore. It matters to me how things are done, what ideas we base our work on, "what ties tie ties,"[2] as Donna Haraway says in *Staying with the Trouble*. I want to pay more attention to how people feel in the process of making something than what is produced. I'm willing to stop, to go back, to move sideways, not to deliver, in order to move at the speed of relationships. I don't want a master, even if he feeds me. I'm willing to bite his hand.

I don't want a master,
even if he feeds me.

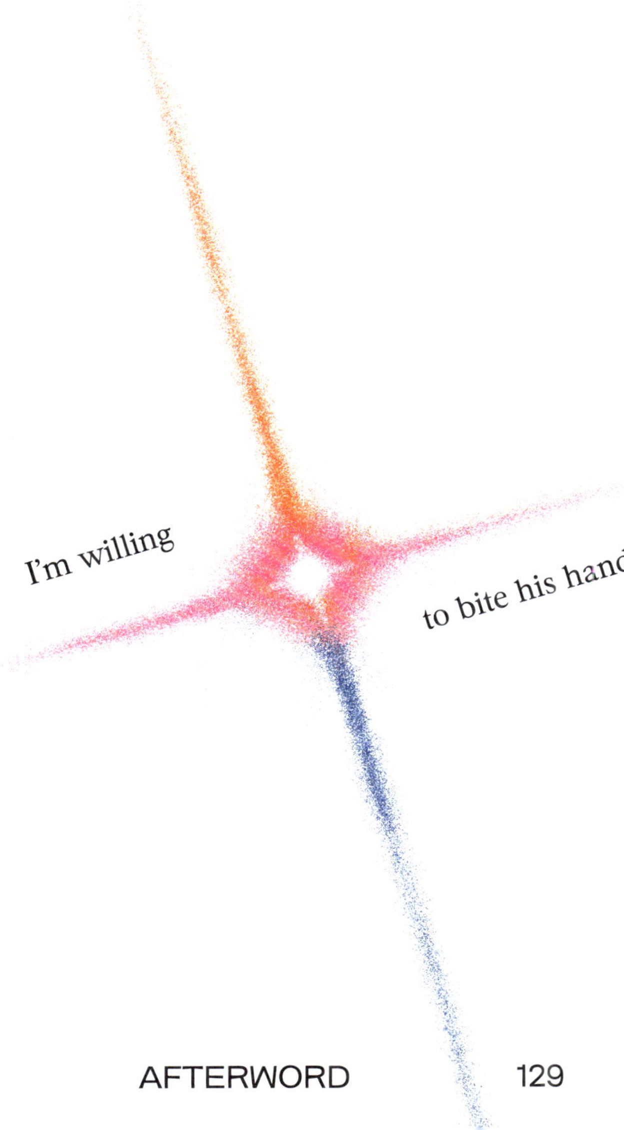

I'm willing
to bite his hand.

NOTES

1 Leanne Betasamosake Simpson, *As We Have Always Done* (University of Minnesota Press, 2020), 48. "*Radical* means a thorough and comprehensive reform, and I use the term in this book to mean root, to channel the vitality of my Ancestors to create a present that is recognizable to them because it is fundamentally different than the one settler colonialism creates. I am not using the term to mean crazy, violent, or from the fringe, nor do I think a trapper's critique of colonialism by setting their traplines is a radical act. It's also normal. It's a valid critique based on direct experience with the system."

2 Donna J. Haraway, *Staying with the Trouble: Making Kin in the Chthulucene* (Duke University Press, 2016), 12.

Thank you to everyone who is making some symbolic attempt at working with radical care as an idea in the academic art world; let's start a social movement and work together to prove our dedication to care over cultural capital. We can use our resumes as ethical bespoke toilet paper as we dare to peer out at what the world needs from us, and not what we have been taught by people who have been made sick by the quick power afforded to them by the gods of capitalist acceleration.

DO IT ANYWAY!

Part Two

DO IT ANYWAY! (Part Two)

ABOUT *THE HOLOGRAM*

The Hologram is a peer-to-peer protocol practiced from beds and couches around the world. It is a practice that anyone can use. The goal of the project is to produce stability for the people who use it. This protocol, when done regularly with focus, produces a rare form of de-institutionalized stability that comes from seeing and being seen, caring and being cared for, and supporting while being supported, in the long-term, by people you know. When you practice it, you are part of building a network of solidarity and trust, outside of profit-driven or otherwise broken institutions. It is not mysterious, nor is it magic. This stability comes from being supported and knowing your friends are supported but not feeling that all that support is your personal responsibility or is coming from a place fueled by capital and exploitation. By making this form of viral communal stability, we believe that hologrammers can and will survive the very scary ends of capitalism together with their communities, and these communities may be able to use their stability to produce new ways of living that don't rely on or reproduce the toxic systems that are killing us.

The Hologram comes from the work produced at the Social Solidarity Clinic of Thessaloniki, in Greece. This is one of about 60 clinics that opened in Greece during their financial crisis (approximately 2008–2015) and a migrant crisis. At the Social Solidarity Clinic of Thessaloniki, where they were already offering free

care, they were also interested in offering care that was better than you would get when you normally went to a traditional doctor, where and when the patient had very little power or agency. Specifically, some members of the clinic team were trying to experiment with how to produce care without the hierarchy that exists between caregivers and care receivers.

When a person came into the clinic, they were no longer referred to as a patient. Instead, they were called an *incomer*. This change in vocabulary tried to minimize the difference in power between, say, the doctor and the person receiving care. The person receiving care is simply coming in from outside, and that's the only difference.

In the Integrative Model, which was the clinic's particular experiment that most influenced the Hologram protocol, the incomer would be seen by a social worker, a therapist, and a general practitioner. All three of these people would ask the incomer questions. The doctor would ask about the body and provide a physical checkup. The social worker might ask about the incomer's financial situation, their work conditions, and their housing. The therapist might ask about the incomer's feelings, their dreams, and their ideas. Each of these care providers could see the questions and answers of the others.

Frosso Moureli, one person who helped develop the Integrative Model, told us that when she was acting as a therapist

alongside a social worker and a doctor, she began to see the incomers as *holograms*—instead of flat pieces of paper—because she could see all their dimensions. That's where we get our unconventional title for this mutual aid project.

The Hologram is a different version of the Integrative Model, done among friends, without experts. We discovered this mutation many years ago in the US, when a few different groups attempted to repurpose the Integrative Model within the cut-throat conditions of the US. This meant that we needed to translate their project without money, without experts or expertise, and without physical space. What was developed is the Hologram protocol as described below.

In *The Hologram*, we refer to the person called the incomer in the Integrative Model in the Social Solidarity Clinic as *the hologram*. This person invites three people who they know to meet with them regularly and ask them questions. One person asks them questions about their mental and emotional health, including feelings and moods, ideas and anxieties, dreams and beliefs. Another friend asks them questions about their social health, including their roommates and family, their relationships, their work, their finances, their relationship to hierarchies, conflicts, and larger social systems. A third friend asks them questions about their physical health, including their body, food, medicine, their home, the planet. These

three people meet with the hologram in one group, and all three ask questions in a structured ritual described below that takes between 90 minutes and two hours. It can happen in person or online.

The hologram is an expert about their own care. Nobody knows how it feels to be them. No one knows what helps or hurts but them, what they've lived through, or what makes them healthy or sick. We also see the hologram as a teacher. Asking for help, being vulnerable, and articulating needs is very unsexy in any of our societies. The hologram shows the other people around them that it's possible and beneficial to clearly ask for the support you need.

The people who ask questions are called *triangle members*. The triangle members' main job is to be openly curious, and to ask the types of questions that help the hologram speak about their pursuit of life. In this way, triangle members are not experts, and they never have to give advice. We think this should feel like a great relief. We know it's hard to resist the temptation to advise or present opinions within our questions. But the triangle members, over time, learn how to use their curiosity and question asking to provide empowering and supportive care to their hologram.

We also see triangle members as critical feelers. We take this idea from disability justice. In the Hologram protocol, triangle members are not trying to fix

any problems. We don't see anyone as a sinking boat whose holes we need to fill or fix. We see each person as someone with wishes who we want to support with curiosity and focused attention. The job of being a critical feeler includes showing curiosity as you try to find out how the hologram feels and why, and to be with them in that without trying to change or fix them.

The triangle members also take notes. When you take notes throughout a session, you sometimes see a linguistic, conceptual, or behavioral pattern that recurs throughout a meeting. If you meet regularly over time, then you can see how certain words or ideas might reappear consistently in someone's life over time. These patterns are really important parts of the process of becoming someone's Living Medical Record.

In the larger project, all caretakers are cared for. The hologram's job is not to give back what they receive from their triangle members, but to ask each of them what kind of support they would like from others, and to help them get it. The hologram might then help one of their triangle members to invite three different people to support them. In this way, the practice spreads, and the hologram may sleep better knowing their friends are cared for, even if they (the hologram) cannot do it for all of them directly.

The hologram who receives support from the three triangle members also

makes someone else a hologram. They do this by becoming a triangle member for someone else (outside of their triangle), along with two other people. This project is based on the idea that supporting somebody else's well-being is a top secret, highly effective medicine that anyone can do well.

ABOUT THIS GUIDE

This guide is for people who want to become holograms and lead sessions where they receive support, based on the model put forth by *The Hologram* project. This guide will help you choose the people to be part of your triangle, and help you set up the group practice. We see this practice as something that comes from an oral tradition, so the best way to learn is from someone else. You can also start out by doing an online workshop, or talking to someone who is already in a Hologram about their experience (email cooperativespecies@gmail.com).

You can adapt the basic principles in this guide to suit your particular group. This guide is geared towards video conference meetings and in person use. If you practice this regularly and would like to share the practice with more people, please read the section called Users' Spell for guidelines on sharing the practice publicly, outside of your friend community.

HOLOGRAM GLOSSARY OF TERMS

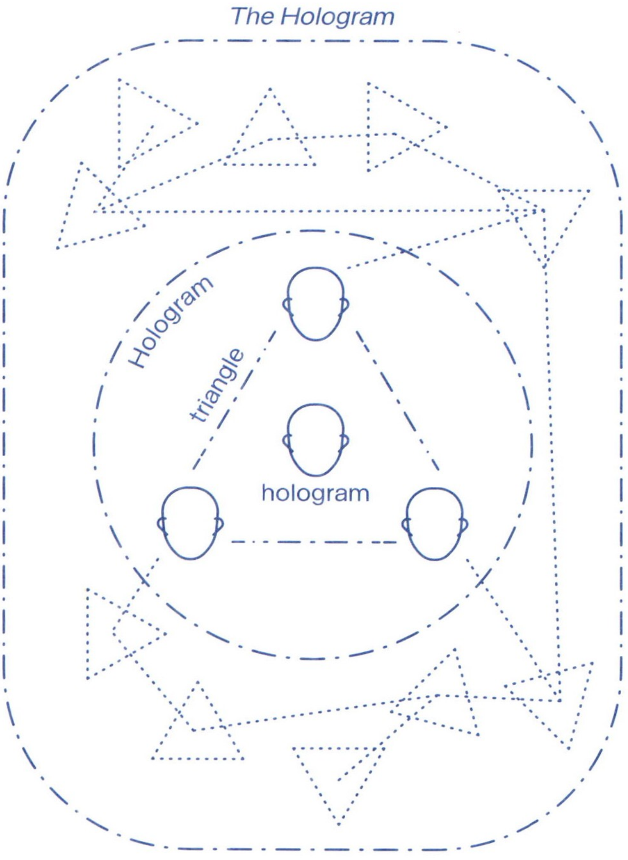

The Hologram This is the overall project, practice, community, and protocol described here. Hopefully it is always changing and growing along with the people who use it.

hologram This is the person who is receiving support from three triangle members through the Hologram protocol.

Hologram This is the group of four people who meet using the protocol outlined below.

triangle This is a group of three triangle members, who meet with a hologram to ask them social, physical, and mental/emotional questions—and to participate in the overall protocol. Over time, the triangle members can become a Living Medical Record (see below) for the hologram.

stuck dance This is a somatic practice we do at the beginning of each Hologram session where everyone gets to reveal how they are stuck. Being stuck in this context can be described by *not knowing what to do*. Have you ever felt like you don't know what to do? Hehe. We have borrowed the stuck dance from Social Presencing Theater, which was developed in part by Arawana Hayashi, and taught to us by Manuela Bosch. As Arawana says on her website, SPT is "a set of practices that synthesize embodied presence, movement theater, stillness, and dialogue"[1] which feels like an academic evolution of Theatre of the Oppressed by Augusto Boal, if you are familiar with that.

To begin the Hologram ritual, each person in the group checks in with a stuck dance. The instructions for how to do the stuck dance are located below within the protocol. Many people see the stuck dance as the best part of the protocol. Even if you feel hesitant about it, we think it is worth giving it a try. You can experiment with it if it doesn't fit you or your group's abilities, styles, or energy levels.

If you do try it, we think you will be very surprised about how much your body can tell your friends, and how well your friends can reflect back to you about the stuckness in your life. Best of all, you may recognize how connected you can feel to yourself and to the group, without relying on words. And it becomes clear that EVERYONE IS STUCK SOMEHOW! (It's *cute!*)

Social Holography This is the lengthiest part of the protocol. During Social Holography, the three triangle members ask the hologram questions. One person asks about social well-being, one about physical well-being, and one about mental and emotional well-being. The questions do not have to happen quickly, or in any order, and follow-ups are welcome. The hologram is free to answer as much as they want, and to say if the questions feel useful to them or not.

reflections Reflections are a part of the protocol that take place after we ask questions using Social Holography. Each of the three triangle members (and also, optionally, the hologram) get to say how they felt during the Hologram so far. Everyone is encouraged to use the phrase, "I felt..." at the beginning of their sentences. One way this practice can work is to offer the hologram a sense of solidarity, where the triangle members reflect back to the hologram what feels familiar, important, or otherwise resonant about

what the hologram has shared. It is fine to share any feelings that came up, as well as personal anecdotes. Reflections are not a chance for the triangle to give advice or share their opinions or analysis about what the hologram said.

feedback In cybernetics, feedback is a process where observations of actions are used as catalysts for further action. In *The Hologram*, feedback is what happens after reflections. Feedback is not advice, but it is a way to give input and energy to the hologram. Feedback comes in three forms: patterns, wishes, and provocations. These three options are described below. Feedback is like a gift, a battery filled with new energy, and a recipe for the hologram to bring home and try out if they want to.

Community of Practice (COPRAC) Community of Practice, sometimes shortened and called COPRAC, is a meeting that anyone interested in or working with *The Hologram* as a practice or idea in their lives can initiate or join. Since April of 2020, COPRAC has happened online. The reason we came up with COPRAC was so that people who started practicing *The Hologram* during a workshop or course could continue to stay in touch with other people they met in those events. At the time of writing, there are three meetings per month online, one in Spanish and two in English. Most people who come are

part of a large chat group on Telegram; information about that can be found on our website (see resource list on page Δ69), assuming you are reading this before 2038. There are more of these meetings that happen locally in cities where many people are learning or practicing *The Hologram*, including Berlin, Zurich, Newcastle upon Tyne, rural New Zealand, and elsewhere by people we don't know.

The process of a COPRAC meeting is simple. Each person introduces themself, and then they express a tension they experience or a question they have about *The Hologram*. When they finish, they invite another person to speak. During this process, it is valuable to take notes and remember the order in which people speak. When everyone has spoken, the first person who spoke begins a new round. In this second round, which goes in the same order as the first round, each person responds to something they heard someone else say. There is no need for advice or expertise, but all help and curiosity is generally welcome. The goal is to try to make sure that everyone who speaks a need or question receives at least a response or acknowledgement in the course of the meeting. After two rounds in a small group, sometimes the group has an extra round if there is extra energy and time. With a large group, it can be a squeeze to fit both rounds into 90 minutes, which is how long the sessions generally are.

In the process, we realized that these meetings allowed Hologram practitioners to support each other to take risks in giving and receiving support, to hack the protocol to make it work for them, and to share resources and techniques along the way. The entire project and protocol benefits greatly from this feedback, which has let us know when some part of the protocol or language was or was not working. Most important, this meeting allows practitioners to feel like they are doing something much more radical than free therapy; this meeting gives most people the sense that they are a part of a new kind of social movement that begins with the way we structure care within the relationships that produce our lives.

Minimum Viable Hologram (MVH)
Minimum Viable Hologram is an online or offline, facilitated, two-hour-long Hologram session also referred to as an MVH. In this session, a peer facilitator will walk you and your chosen triangle through the basic ideas of the project. The peer facilitator can be anyone who has experience using the Hologram protocol. Their role is to explain how each part of the process works and to support your triangle to have a transformative and supportive conversation. You can use this meeting to help you set up your own long-term Hologram or you can just try the practice once. In order to schedule, you will need to invite three people to join you.

social medicine Rooted in the amazing car crash that is industrialization, and whatever we call its ugly social, environmental, and economic aftermath, social medicine as a scientific field gradually began in the early 19th century, during the Industrial Revolution. But we didn't know that back in 2020 when we began to talk about it. We have been talking about *The Hologram* as social medicine, because when you produce a culture of care, where everyone is both giving and receiving support, and stop treating each individual like a lone yacht in the night, entire communities can find stability and move towards some small amount of health (not that health is really a final destination we will ever reach on a burning planet).

Like you, we know that no one on a burning planet is healthy when other people are suffering. Social medicine as a field discusses how social determinants of health impact individual and collective health, disease, and the delivery of medical care. For us in *The Hologram*, that means that no one can be healthy when the people around them are not, which means everyone is sick. It also means that in order to heal ourselves, we need to heal our communities. And in order to do that, we need to abolish the predatory systems like the hierarchical, racist, and profit-driven economic systems we rely on most.

incomer This is the word (replacing the word patient) for the person who is

coming into the Social Solidarity Clinic of Thessaloniki to receive care. Being referred to as an incomer shifts some of the projections commonly made onto a person in need of care, and challenges the hierarchy between doctor and patient.

familiar From Wikipedia:

> In European folklore of the medieval and early modern periods, **familiars** (strictly **familiar spirits**, as "familiar" also meant just "close friend" or companion, and may be seen in the scientific name for dog, *Canis familiaris*) were believed to be supernatural entities, interdimensional beings, or spiritual guardians that would protect or assist witches and cunning folk in their practice of magic, divination, and spiritual insight. According to records of the time, those alleging to have had contact with familiar spirits reported that they could manifest as numerous forms, usually as an animal, but sometimes as a human or humanoid figure, and were described as "clearly defined, three-dimensional ... forms, vivid with colour and animated with movement and sound", as opposed to descriptions of ghosts with their "smoky, undefined form[s]".[2]

For us, we use the term to describe people who are familiar with *The Hologram* practice. We consider someone a familiar after they have practiced twice. When we teach a workshop to incomers, we like to have one familiar in each group of four. They can model and guide the session, making sure that questions stay questions and don't veer towards advice, as well as reminding people of the steps and keeping time.

Living Medical Record This is what you become when you are a long-term member of a hologram's triangle.

United Groundskeepers of Hologram (UGH) An assembly of all Hologram organizers designated to support and push each other. It is a space through which flows most of the organizer knowledge and instincts that people naturally gather as they work on Hologram-related projects. It is there that we share about what it takes to maintain and spread an autonomous health practice. Since 2023, this assembly has also been making all resources and money decisions.

NOTES

1 Arawani Hayashi, "Social Presencing Theater," accessed November 24, 2024, arawanahayashi.com/spt/.

2 "Familiars," Wikipedia, last modified October 29, 2024, en.wikipedia.org/wiki/Familiar.

HOLOGRAM
MANUAL

HOW TO START A HOLOGRAM

First, choose your triangle—three people who will commit to the time and care involved in a Hologram.

Who do you feel the most comfortable with?

Who do you appreciate receiving care from?

Who makes you feel the best about yourself?

Who would you be tickled to see? Who is wise, and fun?

Who have you seen work well with others?

Who asks good questions?

Would the three members of your triangle create a feeling that you would be excited to witness?

How would it feel to enter a room in which they're all together?

Next, invite your three triangle members. *The Hologram* is very different from conventional categories of social relations, including friendships or institutionalized care. You'll be asking your triangle members to play a different role than they normally do in your life (but it is only for small portions of time). Give your potential triangles a call, or start out by adapting this sample letter. Describe what *The Hologram* is, and why you would like them to be involved. Let them know what their participation would mean to you. Share this section of the guide with them, so they understand their role as well as the potential time and emotional commitment.

Invitation Letter Sample

Dear __________ ,

I am writing to ask you to join in an experiment in peer-to-peer healthcare, called *The Hologram*. *The Hologram* has a simple premise: One person (that's me!) invites three trusted people to meet regularly (online or in person), to focus on that person's physical, mental, and social health. It's a way of learning and practicing mutual care, outside or parallel to institutionalized forms of care. *The Hologram* practice was developed by an artist as a way to help distribute the labor of care in a way that can produce stability and health for more people as we survive the end of capitalism and find new ways to thrive collectively.

If this sounds interesting, could you commit to an initial two-hour meeting? At this meeting, I can explain more about *The Hologram* and how it works, and we can try out some of the techniques. The three of you would be part of my "triangle," and you would be there to support me to see myself in all my dimensions. This involves asking me focused questions about my social, physical, or mental/emotional well-being. Your support will help me immensely, and make it possible for me to understand and learn from my present situation.

The Hologram is meant to be a long-term practice, but if you agree, let's just start with one trial meeting. If it feels good to the four of us, it's something we can continue. The goal is, that after you are part of my triangle, I would help you form a triangle of support for yourself.

Thank you so much for hearing me out! It's a little scary to write and ask for this kind of intensive support. I would be very moved if you would be a part of this experiment with me. No matter what your decision is, I hope this leads to future conversations about mutual care.

Yours truly,

____

Now, schedule your first meeting. We suggest that you start with one two-hour meeting. After your first or second meeting you might realize what kind of rhythm and timescale you want to work with. The goal is longevity: What if you were with your group for 10 years?

You could start your Hologram with three meetings over the course of a year. You could also meet seasonally or bimonthly. Be realistic about your time commitment, because you also want to set aside time if the hologram needs support outside of the regular meetings. Being part of a Hologram can be fun, so you might want to meet more often.

MEETING BASICS

You should set aside around two hours for each meeting. If you are having your first meeting outside of a Minimum Viable Hologram (see glossary), the hologram will facilitate.

In the following pages, there's a sample agenda to help you plan for the flow, with detailed descriptions of each item. This can be done online or in person.

~30 min	**PART ONE** Introductions Tech checks Explain *The Hologram* practice Go over the agenda Decide how to record Experiment with pronouns Define and determine roles
~45 min	**PART TWO** Stuck dance Mark the task Asking questions
~35 min	**PART THREE** Reflections Feedback Closing/check-ins Follow-up

1

2

3

1

PART ONE

10 min

Introductions

5 min

Tech checks

10 min

Explain *The Hologram* practice

2 min

Go over the agenda

Δ30

Triangle participants may not know each
other, so do a round of introductions. You
can start with the basics—names, locations,
pronouns. You can also include an icebreaker 1
question "What's the weather like (internal or
external) where you are?"

If you are doing this by video conference or phone, make sure everyone's technology is working. You'll need to be able to see each participant's whole body for later stages, so make sure each person's camera is set up for that.

In your own words, explain the history of *The Hologram*, how the process works, and why we are doing it. You might be able to read to them the earlier section called "About *The Hologram*." The information in that writing is derived from how we usually start a meeting for people trying it for the first time.

You may go over the steps we describe below. It is not completely necessary, but it can be nice for people to know generally what is coming.

2 min

Decide how to record

1

2 min

Experiment with pronouns

Notes are a tool for the future, to remember the past. Decide as a group if someone will take notes or make drawings, or if you'll make an audio or video recording. We recommend that each member take notes on what were the most important moments, 1
statements, or questions for them–these will be helpful in the reflections segment. Well-organized notes are really useful. Decide what you will do with the notes: Will they be shared with the group or kept private, will someone keep them all, under what circumstances could they be shared outside the group (or not at all)?

In Hologram events and workshops, we often use the pronoun "we" when we would usually say "I." First, it causes everyone to slow down when they speak. The more we practice it, the more we observe that saying "we" instead of "I" creates a sense of solidarity in the group—we aren't talking about "your" health, but "our" health—because we know that our health and liberation is bound up in one another's! Try it and see how it affects your group dynamic.

2 min

Define and determine roles

1

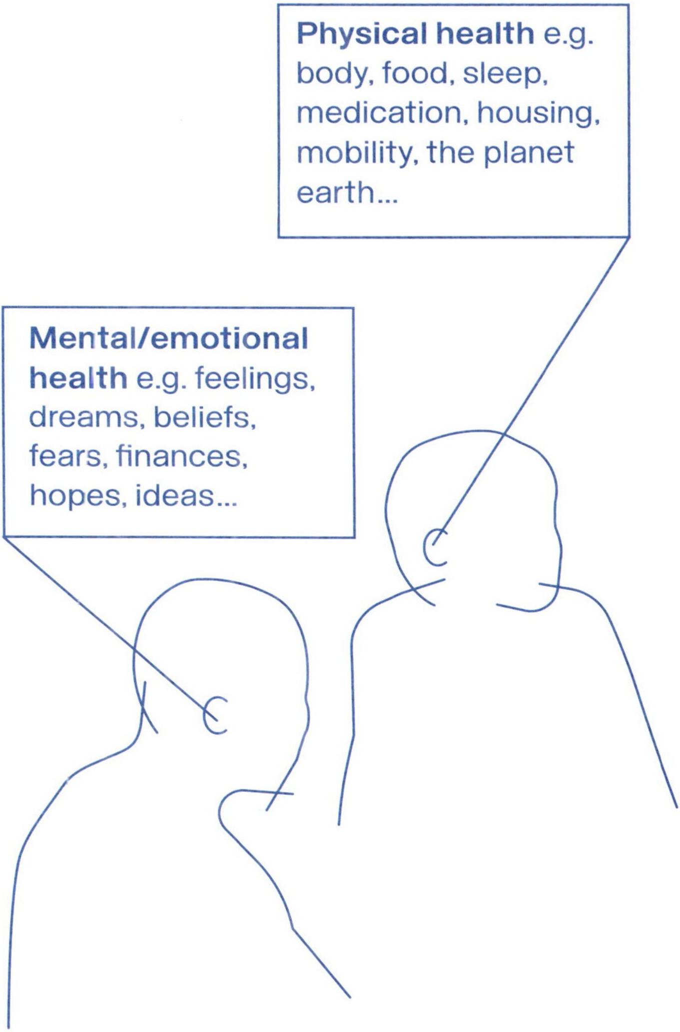

Explain the role of the hologram and the
role of the triangle members. In a triangle,
one person generally asks questions about
the hologram's physical health, one about
social health, and one about mental/emo-
tional health. Decide as a group who will 1
ask what questions. Sometimes it's easiest
for the hologram to determine the roles
ahead of time, with the option for people to
change their roles once things get going.

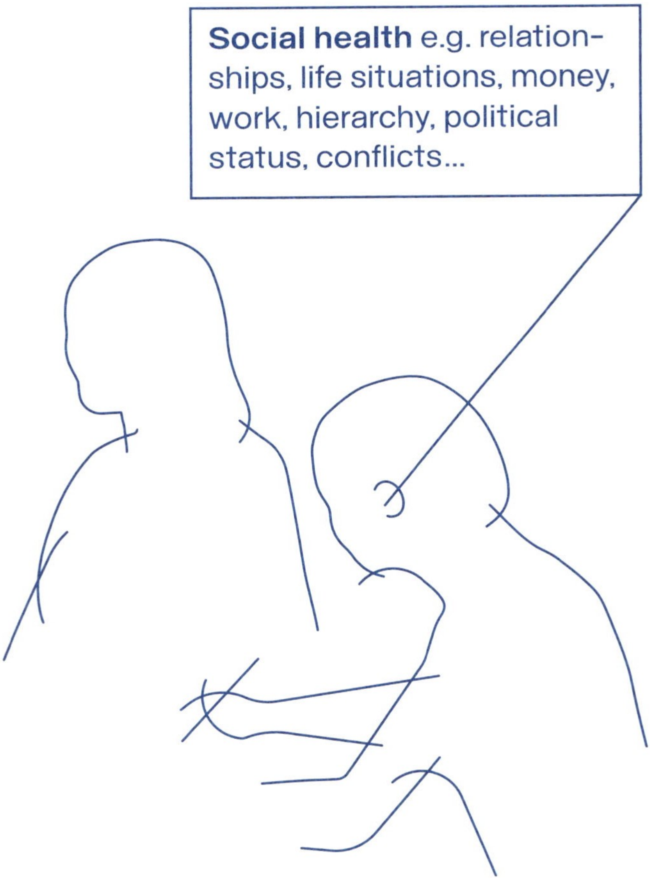

PART TWO

10 min

Stuck dance

2

5 min

Mark the task

The hologram and the triangles all participate in this, with the hologram going last. One at a time, each person positions themselves so they can be seen by the others. They imagine a situation in their life where they feel stuck. They then make a "sculpture" of that feeling with their body and hold it for five seconds. After they come back to the camera, each of the others makes a one to two sentence comment describing what they observed, without any analysis. For example, "I noticed that the sculpture was very soft on the top and very tense on the bottom."

You can also adapt the stuck dance to meet abilities and comfort levels of your group—some people do the stuck dance with only their hand, or with sound. We are always looking for new ideas that promote intimacy, connection, and humor.

The hologram states what they want out of the meeting, including what type of feeling they want to produce for themselves and the group, and what situation they want to talk about. Try to set expectations at the beginning of every meeting. Meetings can be upbeat, fun, focused, and they can provide energy and positivity if you decide to use them that way. If you want to dive deep, or dig up something heavy, be up-front about it with your triangle team so they can prepare.

Asking questions

30 min

2

This is the longest segment of the meeting. The triangle members start by asking questions about what the hologram mentioned when they marked the task, or what came up in their stuck dance. This can be awkward at first–that's okay! You can also ask basic questions to get started, because it's hard to know what the right catalyst for conversation will be. The triangle members don't need to rotate neatly; follow-up questions are welcome. And over time, it becomes normal for the triangle members to ask questions outside of their assigned listening "areas" (social, physical, mental/emotional), as long as it doesn't feel like some part of the hologram is being forgotten. (It can be so easy to narrow down a focus to one problem, like money, and forget about the body, for instance.) It's good to ask follow-up questions, and it's okay if the questions don't lead to a clear conversation, or if there are no apparent solutions.

Questioning simply helps participants explore the hologram's experience without having a goal of changing or fixing anything; it develops question asking skills and helps people learn more about each other.

PART THREE

10 min

Reflections

15 min

Feedback

Start this segment if it feels like enough questions have been asked, or if there's a natural pause in conversation, or if you've run out of time. Each member of the triangle (and the hologram as well) describes what they felt were the most important moments in the conversation. What gave you goosebumps? What felt familiar? What wouldn't you want to forget? This is a chance to feel solidarity with the hologram, as the triangle reveals that some of the feelings and experiences described in the session are things they find familiar. It can be such a relief to feel like you are not alone!

Take five minutes to write down some feedback for the hologram (the hologram can give themselves feedback too). Feedback is not advice. Instead, it is based on the observations that happened within the session. The feedback can include:

1. **Patterns:** Mention if you noticed a pattern in the language or behavior of the hologram. Just describing the pattern is enough. No analysis necessary.

2. **Wishes:** Make a wish for the hologram based on what you learned. What do you hope for them? Detailed wishes are 3
the best.

3. **Provocation:** Give the hologram a prompt: "what if you were to..."

10 min

Closing/check-ins

Follow-up

in the days or weeks following the session

3

You can create a closing ritual to make sure there is clarity, closure, and peace in the group. This could be a breathing, movement, or listening exercise. One person has invented an *UN*stuck dance that usually involves everyone dancing and shaking together. Afterwards, discuss how everyone is feeling after the session. What are they going to do after the call or gathering? Do we want to do this again? This may be a time to decide on next steps.

Decide who will write a follow-up email. This could include a summary of the meeting, an invitation to plan the next one, a list of questions to think about before then, or the start of a conversation about how the group would like to move forward.

Note: In our experience, it works well to have one to three meetings before setting "guidelines" or trying to make big group decisions. It may take a few sessions to learn how the group works together and what *The Hologram* practice feels like, before the group feels comfortable making plans or decisions. Once you get there, you could plan a meeting where you do one hour of hologramming, and one hour of setting group agreements. At this time, you can make a list of questions to discuss such as these:

* How will we schedule our meetings?
* How long is this experiment going to last? Three months? Two years?
* When and how will we check in about the group process and make amendments?
* How will we deal with conflicts or difficult feelings?
* What happens if someone wants to leave the group?

FAQS AND TIPS FOR TRIANGLES

You might feel excitement and anxiety when you are asked to be a triangle member! These questions and tips can help you learn more about the experience.

FREQUENTLY ASKED QUESTIONS

*** Why did this person ask me?**
Holograms choose triangle members for all kinds of reasons. They are people they trust, whose opinions they admire, who make them feel safe, who make them laugh and feel joyful, and/or who have a particular understanding or knowledge of them. In asking you to be a triangle, the hologram thinks highly of you and is asking for support.

*** What are my responsibilities?**
The hologram is at the center of the triangle. They are in charge of the process, convening it, and setting the mission of the group. It is the job of the three people in the triangle to commit, to listen, to remember, and to reflect back. Each triangle listens to and asks questions around one specific theme: physical health, social health, and emotional health. Over time, they will begin to notice patterns that the hologram themself may not be able to see. Each H/hologram is different, but you might expect these responsibilities:

- To agree to support your hologram until you decide together to end the support

- To attend sessions
- To actively listen during sessions
- To follow the agreed-upon structure of the session, including withholding judgments and refraining from giving advice
- To ask clarifying and challenging questions based on the role that your hologram gives you (to pay attention to their social, emotional, or physical health)
- To notice things about your hologram, for example, what they communicate verbally and non-verbally, consciously and unconsciously, including patterns that you notice over time
- To cooperate with and be supportive of your fellow triangle members
- To keep careful and non-incriminating notes that would never put the hologram in danger, so that you can safely keep track of what is happening over time
- To take care of yourself and your needs, and set your own boundaries
- To keep what your hologram shares in confidence, unless they agree that you can share it

∗ What's in it for me?

Most triangle members find their role incredibly rich and nourishing. It feels good to feel needed and helpful, and very often listening to someone else's struggles sheds new light on—and helps us connect with—our own. However, your hologram

should not reciprocate by listening back to you in the same way. Instead, their role includes helping you to set up your own Hologram or other support system when you feel ready.

*** I'm not a health expert–what if I don't know what to do?**
None of us are experts, and at the same time all of us are. Society teaches us to be suspicious of and to undermine ourselves and each other. We hope *The Hologram* practice can put us back in touch with dormant skills and instincts for supporting each other. But in truth, no triangle member knows what to do at first! And every hologram's needs are different. If you simply listen to your hologram and follow their lead, and listen to yourself, there is very little you can "get wrong."

If you need more guidance, your hologram can set up a Minimum Viable Hologram (MVH), in which an outside facilitator guides you through a sample session.

*** What if the session gets too intense?**
A certain amount of discomfort is normal in a session–it shows you're pushing through imagined obstacles and doing good work! It's very normal for any triangle member to feel a momentary stomach lurch that signals "I can't manage this!" If you need to hold back, most likely one of your fellow triangle members will be able to take the lead in that moment. The Hologram form is not a replacement

for therapy—sessions are best used to answer questions of the present and the future rather than the past. If the conversation is going down a route you feel you and your fellow triangle members are unable to manage, you could ask a question that brings your hologram back to the present moment, or transforms the emotional place they are in. You can also take a moment to check in with each other by asking, "How are we feeling right now?" or, "Is this a good moment to take a minute break?"

✻ What if I get triggered in a session?
It is important to set your own boundaries and listen to yourself in a session. Sometimes a hologram can knowingly or unknowingly raise something about themselves that relates directly to something you have experienced. This can be emotionally painful, but can also be validating and connecting. Listen to your needs and if you don't feel okay for any reason, we encourage you to voice this to the others. You can decide together whether you wish to stay in the meeting and change the subject, take a time out, or end the session. If you are worried about specific triggers, we suggest discussing this in advance with the group, and deciding together how to protect each other from harm or exhaustion.

✻ What if I feel too exhausted or hopeless or busy or I don't like the other

triangle members or it isn't working for me for some other reason?
Many people find that being a triangle is a life-affirming and enjoyable experience from which they gain a lot personally, especially if they have their own support systems set up. If, in listening to your own needs you realize that you can no longer support your hologram, let them know as soon as possible with as much care, respect, and honesty as possible. You can even support them to find someone to take your place. We suggest that, early in the process, the group comes to an agreement about endings, so that a person's departure can be as supportive as possible.

✳ **Will the triangle ever meet without the hologram present?**
It's a different kind of labor if you are meeting outside of the Hologram protocol to discuss the person you are supporting. Think about and discuss if, or when, this could be useful to the group, and how does everyone (including the hologram themselves) feel about it?

TIPS FOR TRIANGLE MEMBERS DURING SESSIONS

✳ **Trust in yourself.** If you have an instinct, follow it, and don't second-guess yourself. Have compassion for yourself. It's

very normal to feel unsure about something, and is probably a sign that you want to do the best for your hologram.

✱ **Remember that during the session, the focus should be on the hologram.** Your role is to listen and to ask questions, rather than share your own experience or responses. You can note these, however, and return to them for the reflections and feedback segments.

✱ **Try to ensure that each triangle member gets to ask a good number of questions.** Be mindful that other triangle members might be less confident about speaking up. You might ask a couple of questions, and then leave space for the others to step in when they are ready. Having a bit of quiet space between questions can be very useful.

✱**Silences are important.** If you find you don't have a question at the moment, don't worry! Silences can help the hologram do some thinking, and your fellow triangle members might be cooking up an amazing question! It is also perfectly acceptable to need time to process what you hear before asking a question.

✱ **It's fine if your question doesn't directly relate to your role (e.g., physical, emotional, social).** Triangle members' roles can merge slightly, as long as all bases are covered in a session. If you

notice another triangle moving into another role, you can help rebalance by asking a question relating to their role.

* **Listen to yourself.** Notice your emotional state, whether it is joy or sadness or anger. This can be helpful for you or your hologram to hear during the reflections segment. If something feels uncomfortable or harmful, make sure you take care of your own needs, as that is an important part of showing good support for your hologram.

* **Take notes in a way that makes sense to you!** These can be written, drawn, doodled, short-hand, and/or in multicolor. Note-taking will enrich your capacity to notice patterns.

* **Reflect back what you are feeling.** You will have the chance to share direct reflections at the end of the session, but if you see your hologram feeling anxious or self-conscious before that, it can be incredibly reassuring for them to hear something reaffirming like, "That feels familiar," or "We connect a lot with that."

* **Remember that this should be a learning and nourishing experience for you as well as your hologram**, so do what you need to do before, during, or after a session to make it as fulfilling as possible for you as well.

THE STATE OF *THE HOLOGRAM* PRACTICE IN 2024

The Hologram is a practice that anyone can do. But it is also a community.

We ran the numbers about what it would mean if 1,000 people practice the Hologram protocol through one of our offerings: attending a course, reading the book, taking part in a peer-facilitated session or a workshop. If every 10th person formed their own Hologram even temporarily at some point, it would mean that there would be 1,300 people who have tried it. If every 50th person from those 1,300 people carries on hologramming for a while, to the point that their triangle members find their own three people to form a Hologram, another 100 people join the community of practitioners. If a third of this second generation also establishes their own Holograms, we might be looking at 500,000 new Hologram familiars next year, just from the protocol's viral nature. Of course we won't actually see most of those people practicing. They will have tried the practice and either taken it and made it their own, or it might lay dormant in their stash of care and survival skills until it's time. We think that about 200 million people will be doing it soon.

There are currently three monthly meetups, called Community of Practice, for anybody who is interested in or already practicing the Hologram protocol. They take place online. Two of them are in English and one is in Spanish. They are facilitated by volunteers. Information about this is on our website.

Volunteer seasoned practitioners also facilitate so-called Minimum Viable Hologram sessions (see glossary). Anybody who would like to try *The Hologram* can sign up with their three triangle members for this two-hour long call. A volunteer will then walk them through the basics and be there while they practice for the first time, making it easy to start one's own Hologram. The rotating cast of volunteers is made up of people who want to become facilitators of the protocol so they can bring it to their own community.

At least once a year (and in the past more frequently), three Hologram organizers decide to facilitate a course. Between 2020 and 2024, we have run eight courses, each offering a deep dive into the ideas behind the protocol, each with a slightly different focus: for instance, one in Spanish, about mothering; one for informal caregivers; another one for people identifying with masculinity; a different one focusing on difficult collaborations in collective organizing. We have also tried many other experiments, such as workshops for people who share a certain medical diagnosis, introducing the protocol to workers in a clinic for migrants, running a "school" of different mutual aid practices in Berlin, using the protocol to shake up tech startups, and so much more. All these offerings were and always are free, as we believe nobody should ever pay for hologramming.

Our biggest experiment so far has been the project's decentralization, which is an ongoing process. In early 2023, we established the United Groundskeepers of Hologram (UGH): an assembly of all Hologram organizers designated to support and push each other. It is a space through which flows most of the knowledge and instincts that people naturally gather as they work on Hologram-related projects. It is there that we share about what it takes to maintain and spread an autonomous health practice. Since 2023, this assembly has also been making all resources and money decisions.

It is the systems that are broken, not us. We are here to become stable and healthy so that we have the energy and capacity to destroy the systems that harm us, and dream of new ones.

Everyone is invited to use *The Hologram* as a practice for individual and collective transformation, for the redistribution of care, and to learn.

Next we share a list of guidelines for sharing *The Hologram* outside your own community. If you are imagining teaching or offering *The Hologram* to people outside of your own triangle, family, or friends—in other words, if you are in any way publicly (re)presenting *The Hologram*—treat this as a user's license.

USERS' SPELL

The Hologram is an open-source protocol free to use in your own life and in your community of friends. If you want to spread _The Hologram_ to a wider public, you can treat this as a users' license.

All of us who teach *The Hologram* also practice *The Hologram* and have a triangle of our own. There are at least three reasons for this. First, it is very important that we understand the protocol in all its complexity—how it feels and works best for us—and that when we speak about it, we can share firsthand experience. We also believe that if we are not ready to be a hologram, we are not ready to share the project. Third, this viral social practice should be spread from practitioner to practitioner, allowing it to morph and change through use. We recommend that we use the practice proportionally more than we discuss it in abstraction. When we are practicing a lot then we are less at risk of over-theorizing and thus losing the point.

Sharing, facilitating, or teaching *The Hologram* is a chance to share what we have developed as much as it is a chance to learn, to collaborate, to find solidarity, and to build networks. When we present *The Hologram*, it is an opportunity to learn and ask questions, just like we do in the practice. It is a great excuse to invite an avalanche of very magical and practical information about how other people are organizing survival and thriving in the

racial Capitalocene. In other words, there is no place for dogma, top-down authority, or ego boosting. Just like in the practice, everyone is always curious, no one is an expert, and the person who needs support is the teacher.

All profit created by the sharing of *The Hologram* (social capital, financial capital, access to community or good energy) should be redistributed after we use what we need. We believe that by redistributing resources they will multiply.

The Hologram can always be used as a way to explore people's unspoken needs in a given situation and to help guide the redistribution of resources, including money, work, energy, and joy. We think money is a strange experiment that hasn't worked super well for most humans doing wage labor in a system that profits off their death. That's why generally, *The Hologram* hates money. That's also why we are not afraid to do our part to ruin the economy and our habits within it by paying people to try *The Hologram* for the first time (this is something we did when we had foundation money). We are literally buying their time away from wage labor so they can feel what care can be outside of money's utopia.

While we pay a living wage to the project's workers and are developing ways to do that for more people, we don't ever want to become a business. Nor do we want to be used by those with interest in financial profit.

We certainly don't ever want anyone to be charged to learn, experience, build, or practice *The Hologram*. No Hologram events or experiences should ever cost any individual money (no matter how rich they are) though we are happy to accept and redistribute institutional funds. *The Hologram* is a gift we give each other, and it must remain so as we imagine our way out of the delusions of capital, one gift at a time.

When it is truly practiced with focus, attention, and time, *The Hologram* will naturally destroy any corporation (like Amazon, Apple, Google, The Museum of Modern Art, or an Ivy League university). The honesty and solidarity produced in the practice will naturally erode power structures and destroy harmful systems of reality maintenance.

The Hologram is for everyone. However, we the facilitators and organizers of *The Hologram* are a relatively small group of people, so we cannot provide support to everyone at once. Thus, when deciding where to put our holographic light beams of energy, we believe that prioritizing the care of people who are hurt most by systems of oppression should come before offering to support the well-being of people with power. While we think that workers could and should make the boss a hologram and witness their vulnerability, we believe that the workers themselves should be stable and healthy, as should be their caretakers, before we labor to help the boss.

The Hologram and any events or projects that are related to it are based first and foremost on the creation of relationships, solidarity, and health. For this reason, decisions for or plans about *The Hologram* happen strategically slowly in a way that multiplies these three things:

1. When planning events, meetings, or other manifestations, we always wait for everyone who wants to be there.
2. We move at the pace of our relationships which means that we wait for people to be ready, for communication to be clear, for trust to be present.
3. We don't feel rushed by institutional deadlines or some inherited sense of efficiency or speed.

When we share *The Hologram*, our goal is to offer enough structure, clarity, support, and information about why the practice exists and how it works so that participants feel grounded and supported enough to take the practice and make it what they want it to be. We want people to feel excited and inspired to try it and play with it and make it their own, and we strive to create the conditions that support that.

The projects and workshops that come out of *The Hologram* are a gift and should be treated as something very special, from somewhere deep in the earth. We can treat the manifestations of *The Hologram* how we would like to treat other gifts that emerge from the earth—like water, like trees, or like life itself—with curiosity and care.

When we are doing the labor of facilitation and organizing, we should celebrate and care for ourselves as a part of this amazing care package that emerged from and for the world. We share information and energy that we collect through *The Hologram* back to the project's ancestors, to make sure our energy bank is full and we can know our work is not useless.

We invite people with power over us to practice *The Hologram* and see if they continue to want their power.

A NOTE ON PROCESS

In 2021 Cassie Thornton began work on an exhibition. The exhibition was about *The Hologram*, a mutual aid project developed by Cassie and friends since 2016. The exhibit was located at the National Museum of Psychology in Akron Ohio, and it portrayed the bedroom of a person living in COVID-19 lockdown, who had been studying *The Hologram*. As Cassie prepared the exhibit with the curatorial team, they also practiced *The Hologram* together and separately. Many of the objects being exhibited were sourced from the curators Fran Ugalde's and Jenn Bazar's homes, so Cassie's research visits included going home with Fran to take stuff from her mom's garage and looking through Jenn's personal collection of homemade masks. The exhibition opened in July of 2023, and the museum allowed the exhibit to stay up almost a full year; it closed in May of 2023. It was a long run and an excellent immersive exhibition, but most of the global Hologram community did not get to see it.

At the closing of the exhibition, Cassie proposed to make a catalog about it. However, making a catalog at the closing of an exhibition didn't make sense to anybody besides her. Without funding, a publisher, or a mode of distribution, Cassie worked on the project very slowly. Months after the closing of the exhibition, Cassie asked her friend and fellow hologrammer Eleonora Toniolo if she would design the book. Cassie wrote like a snail

and Ele curated the images and evolved the design as Cassie slithered. The two first decided to produce the catalogue as a very simple and graphic object that allowed people to quickly understand the exhibition and *The Hologram* practice. They imagined that the book would be in two parts, and that the second part would include a very simple manual for how to practice *The Hologram*, which had already been written by Cassie with Lita Wallis, and honed by many hologrammers over the past years, but which was not yet officially published.

A year into the book project, all three curators contributed writings, and the book began to take shape. But by then, Cassie and Ele began to second guess the potential of this book. Do we have space for coffee table books in the apocalypse? What can this "too late" exhibition guide do? Who will even see it if we don't have a publishing plan? In need of a bit more fiery energy and support, Cassie and Ele then invited a friend and collaborator named Magda Härtelova to contribute her eyes and two writings to the book. Magda had already been writing a book about the difference between curating and caring, and was plenty impatient with the art world for many reasons you can now read about. In order to get started with the writing, Magda invited three curators, Ruth Catlow, Prem Krishnamurthy and Amanda Nudelman, to do a Hologram for her in the year 2038 about curating.

Finally it became clear that the book was becoming a critical offering to utopian cultural workers trying to make art in the apocalypse. The occasion of publishing the exhibition guide was to present *The Hologram* as a practice to people in the art world who felt stuck doing more theorizing and exhibiting of ideas than life-changing practices. When Magda's two writings seemed to complete this little book, Cassie, Ele and Magda brought the project to the central organizing assembly behind *The Hologram* to ask for their eyes, blessings, and some financial support for the project. And they gave it. With this funding Cassie also reached out to her sci-fi hologrammer friend Heather Kapplow to help weave together all the mysterious, holographic time traveling texts together, and months of tiny edits began. Around this time, Cassie got enough confidence in the book to get in touch with Erin Segal from Thick Press, who responded with so much affirmation, generosity, and clarity. We've been weaving, sensemaking, and playing with the commas of the time-traveling texts together ever since...

RESOURCES AND CONTACT

PRINT

English book
The Hologram: Feminist, Peer-to-Peer Health for a Post-Pandemic Future, by Cassie Thornton
(to order) plutobooks.com

Greek translation
Χόλογκραμ: μια φεμινιστική πρακτική για ένα μέλλον συλλογικής υγείας, της Κασι Θορντον
(to order) periplanetabooks.com

Spanish translation
Holograma: Salud feminista entre pares para un futuro postcapitalista, de Cassie Thornton
(to download) craterinvertido.org

DIGITAL

Hologram website
thehologram.xyz

Email
cooperativespecies@gmail.com

Telegram chat
t.me/+Vqvi3__V1F0aW7jG

Support *The Hologram*
opencollective.com/the-hologram